J. L. Scott

The Pourtraicture of his Sacred Majestie in his Solitudes and Sufferings

J. L. Scott

The Pourtraicture of his Sacred Majestie in his Solitudes and Sufferings

ISBN/EAN: 9783337143497

Printed in Europe, USA, Canada, Australia, Japan

Cover: Foto ©ninafisch / pixelio.de

More available books at **www.hansebooks.com**

Εἰκὼν Βασιλικὴ.

THE

POURTRAICTURE

OF

HIS SACRED MAJESTIE

IN

HIS SOLITUDES AND SUFFERINGS.

A

REPRINT OF THE EDITION OF 1648,

AND

A FACSIMILE OF THE ORIGINAL FRONTISPIECE,

WITH AN INTRODUCTION THROWING FRESH LIGHT
UPON THE AUTHORSHIP OF THE WORK

BY

EDWARD J. L. SCOTT, M.A., OXON.,
Assistant Keeper of MSS., British Museum.

LONDON:
ELLIOT STOCK, 62, PATERNOSTER ROW. E.C.
1880.

PREFACE.

THE history of *Eikon Basilike* has been so often written, and the merits and capabilities of the two persons to whom the authorship has been attributed for producing such a work have been so fully tested and considered by their various supporters on either side, that it may seem unnecessary and almost impertinent to attempt to say anything on so threadbare a subject. But the latest writer who has given an opinion on the case carries such weight in his name, and is so likely to be accepted as an authority on this point, that it is all the more to be desired that his views, if incorrect, should be challenged, and where possible refuted. In a monograph on Milton, just issued, for the series of English Men of Letters, is a brief account in four pages of *Eikon Basilike*, wherein are reproduced all the blunders and misstatements which it was the laborious task of Dr. Wordsworth, fifty years ago, to expose and confute. Indeed, his masterly letters to the Archbishop of Canterbury might as well have never been written, and he might have spared himself the trouble of replying to Todd, Broughton, Lingard, Hallam, and the rest of his able and ingenious opponents. We are told once more in direct terms that *the book was composed by Dr. Gauden.* Of this, however, no proof is adduced, but the writer adds that *it is possible that Gauden may have had in his hands some written scraps of the King's meditations.* This is rather in favour of the King, as it allows him some original meditations, a point generally contested by his enemies, and very damaging to Gauden, because the latter distinctly denies that he owed anything whatever to his rival; the book and figure, he says, being wholly and only his own invention, making, and design. We are told on the next page that *though a Royalist, Gauden sat in the Westminster Assembly.* If this be so, how comes Professor Masson, in his exhaustive list of the men who composed that Assembly, to have omitted the name of so distinguished a *Royalist* (there were not many, it may be imagined, of that class in that august body) as Gauden? And further, *he took the Covenant, for which compliance he nearly lost the reward which after the Restoration became his due.* If there is one point about Gauden which is doubtful, it is whether he ever took the Covenant; and he is believed to have denied that he did so. *The readers of Eikon Basilike never doubted that the meditations were those of the royal martyr.* What becomes then of the first controversy which raged so fiercely in 1649 as to the authorship of the book, and which produced so many pamphlets on both sides for and against the King, such as the "Princely Pelican" and many others? Two pages further on we are told that *the plagiarism of the prayer from Sidney's "Arcadia" ought to have opened Milton's eyes to the unauthentic character of the Eikon.* What had a subsequent appendix to the *Eikon* (the prayers being no part of the first edition, but added afterwards to later ones) to do with the authentic character of a work of which at the time of publication they formed no portion? *The secret of the authorship of the "Eikon" was well kept, being known only to a very few persons—the two royal brothers, Bishop Morley, the Earl of Bristol, and Clarendon.* If we are to believe Gauden's own words, the only one of these persons who knew it was Bishop Morley, and he, as I shall shortly prove, never for one moment attributed the work to any but Charles I., from the date of its appearance in 1649 to his death in 1684. It is true that Gauden frequently appealed to Morley's knowledge of it, but there is not a word from Morley to prove that he knew it. Gauden plainly tells us that *the two royal brothers* first learnt the secret from himself in the end of 1660, and that he was not made a Bishop on that account, a fact which Mrs. Gauden is also equally positive about; and yet we are now told *he pleaded it successfully as a claim to preferment at the Restoration, and he received the bishopric of Exeter.* Why, so far different is the truth, that he was actually nominated as a fit person to fill a see in 1658, two years before he ever made his claim at all. Clarendon and Bristol both, according to Gauden's own letters, are made acquainted with the secret after the Restoration, when he is already Bishop of Exeter. Such is the latest account of the *Eikon Basilike*, and of the circumstances attending its production; but as all these points have long ago been satisfactorily cleared up and settled by Dr. Wordsworth, it is only necessary now, in writing a Preface for a New Edition, to bring before the notice of the public any fresh evidence which may have turned up during the last fifty years. As Dr. Wordsworth confidently prophesied at the close of his labours that such evidence would come to light in the course of time, and that it would be wholly for the King and against Gauden, so his prophecy has been verified to a great extent, and will no doubt some day be completely fulfilled. There are two grounds on which this question has generally been disputed: 1st, the internal; 2nd, the external evidence. On both these heads something new may be said; and 1st, as to the internal. To begin with the title page. It has never been noticed that while the first edition has the date "MDCXLVIII." alone, all later editions before 25th March, 1649 have the words "Reprinted in R[egis] M[emoriam] 1648." This is strong evidence in support of the statement that the *Eikon* was first *printed* (but not published) during the King's life. This is one point against Gauden, for his wife declares that he could not get it printed until *some few days after* the King's death. If Charles I. was dead at the time of the printing of the title page of the *Eikon*, that work could not have been entitled the Portraiture of his Majesty, but of his *late* Majesty.

Next, as to the frontispiece. Here there are three or four new points to be noticed. The emblems in it are taken from different parts of the *Eikon* itself, such as the crowns of gold and of lead, from the end of Chapter VI.; the metaphor of the sea raging when stormy winds blow upon it, from Chapter IV.; and many others. Next, the verses beneath the frontispiece, being the explanation of it, bear the signature G. D., which Todd explains to mean G[auden] D[esigned], or G[auden], D[ean of Bocking]. But Dr. Wordsworth, on the other hand, says these initials must stand for G[ulielmus] D[ugard], the printer of one edition of the *Eikon;* and that he is right in so saying is proved by the discovery of the diary (now in the British Museum, Add. MS. 23,146) of Dugard's brother Thomas, who throughout it uses that remarkable and striking capital D, which is also found in Dugard's earlier edition of the *Eikon*. This copy is now in the hands of the Rev. Thomas Ford Fenn, Head Master of Trent College, near Nottingham. In another early copy, of 1648[9], from Dugard's press, in the possession of Mrs. Manson, of Muswell Hill, these explanatory verses are not *printed*, but *engraved* from the handwriting of their author, and bear no shadow of resemblance to Gauden's hand, but are written in the style of a schoolmaster's copies; and William Dugard was High Master of St. Paul's Grammar School. Again, it has not been noticed that the Greek motto at the foot of the frontispiece, τὸ χῖ οὐδὲν ἠδίκησε τὴν πόλιν οὐδὲ τό κάππα, which Gauden, in his sermon on the 30th January, 1648[9], refers to Constantine, has really no reference whatever to that Emperor, but to Constantius, for Julian the Apostate, from whose *Misopogon* this line is quoted, is speaking of the time when he himself was made Cæsar. This sermon directly attributes the *Eikon* to Charles I.; and it is absolutely impossible that Gauden, the writer of it, should have misunderstood and misapplied the quotation which, as Gauden, the author of the *Eikon*, he had made use of only a year before. Another point on which great stress has been laid by both parties in their arguments is the fact that the first couplet of the explanation of the frontispiece presents the very words in English which in Latin close the *Eikon*, viz., "*Vota dabunt quæ bella negarunt,*" and that this Latin motto is found at the end of a poem called "Majesty in Misery," composed by Charles I. at Carisbrook. But no one has apparently noticed that all three come from one and the same place, viz., the concluding words of Chapter XVIII. of the *Eikon* itself, "What we could not get by our treaties we may gain by our prayers." Consequently, as the verses appear first in Dugard's edition of the frontispiece, so does the motto at the close of his edition, being, no doubt, added by himself. The truth is that this comparison of the various editions of the work has never hitherto been attempted, and yet, if closely followed up, would inevitably lead to most important results as to the real authorship. Let all copies now known to exist be collected together, and collated carefully one with another, and who can say what further evidence would not instantly be elicited, which might set this unhappy question at rest for ever. The British Museum alone possesses twenty-five copies, the Lambeth Library four, and so on, many of which contain manuscript notes and memoranda hitherto unpublished. There is one piece of internal evidence in favour of

Charles I. which has never yet been adduced, and that is a comparison of the apophthegmata in the *Eikon* with those composed by the King, and written with his own hand in his copy of Bacon's *Advancement of Learning* (interpreted by Gilbert Wats, Oxford, 1640), now in the British Museum. This book is exhibited under glass in a case in the King's library, and yet has remained all these years unnoticed and unquoted. They are so very important that the whole of them are subjoined here in order that future readers of the *Eikon* may find out the parallel passages for themselves. They occur in Book VI., pp. 300—323, where examples of the Antitheta are given under various headings, *pro et contra*, such as Nobility, Beauty, Youth, &c.

HEALTH IV.

Pro.

"None so truly knowes the value of Healthe as those who want it."

PRAISE REPUTATION IX.

Pro.

"Reward is nothing but reall Praise."

LIFE XII.

Pro.

"If long Lyfe were not a great Blessing, God had neuer offerd it as a reward to Mankynde."

SUPERSTITION XIII.

Pro.

"If a Man, by eschewing superstition, grow to be Profaine, what hath he gotten?"

PRIDE XIV.

Contra.

"Pride made Angels Deuils."

Envy XVI.
Contra.
"All Enuy proceeds from a knowen selfe unworthiness."

Cruelty XVIII.
Contra.
"None but Cowards are cruell."

Vainglory XIX.
Contra.
"Vaine glorious Persons are neuer satisfied, though they obtaine what they desyer, as thinking their Merit beyond theire owen imagination."

Fortitude XXI.
Pro.
"A feareful Man wants but occasion to be Vitius."

Temperance XXII.
Pro.
"Temperance rewards a man when he least thinks of it."

Constancy XXIII.
Contra.
"Varietie is this World's delight."

Magnanimity XXIV.
Contra.
"How can that be a Virtue which is built upon Vyce?"

Knowledge Contemplation XXV.
Pro.
"Knowledge giues lyke Pleasure to the Mynde wch Venus doth to the Body."

Learning XXVI.
Pro.
"Naturall Witt, destitute of Learning, is but lyke unpolished Marble."

Loquacity XXXI.
Contra.
"Few great Talkers are good Doers."

Boldnesse XXXIII.
Contra.
"None but Fooles or ill-bred Men are Impudent."

Jeasts XXXV.
Contra.
"Dull jesters are contemned, & those who are witty are more hated then praised."

Love XXXVI.
Pro.
"Love is the Mother of all noble Actions."

Innovation XL.
Pro.
"[He that will not apply new remedies] must neuer cure new Diseases."

Contra.
"He that Innouats hath need to be verry Wyse, for he taxes all Men of Ignorance."

Violent Consils XLIV.
Contra.
"Nothing but a desperat Disease can tollerat a violent Remedy."

Suspicion XLV.
Contra.
"Suspition is incompatible with true frendship. Suspition allwais proceedeth eather from Feare or Gilt."

All these apophthegms strike one on reading them at first as extremely similar in style and expression to those scattered throughout the pages of the *Eikon;* for instance, at the beginning of Chapter XVI. of that work occurs the following sentence: "So hardly can the pride of those that study novelties allow former times any share or degree of wisdom or godliness." Compare with this the entry by Charles with his own hand in Bacon's work under the head of Innovation, "He that Innovats hath need to be verry Wyse, for he taxes all men of Ignorance." To sum up, therefore, the new evidence in favour of the King and against Gauden, gathered from the internal proofs, we have:—1st, The inference (from the title-page of the King not being styled his *late* Majesty, coupled with the simple date, "1648," in place of "Reprinted in Regis Memoriam. 1648;") that the book was printed during his lifetime, the Gauden story being that it was not printed until *after* his death. 2nd, The fact of the frontispiece being the representation of various metaphors in the pages of the work, a point to which Gauden never alludes in support of his claim to be the author of both book *and* figure. 3rd, The explanation of the letters G. D. at the foot of the verses to be Gulielmus Dugard, not Gauden Designed, or Gauden, Dean of Bocking. 4th, The true origin of the line, "If prayers can give me what the wars deny," or "*Vota dabunt quæ bella negarunt,*" to be found in Chapter XVIII. of the *Eikon*. 5th, The handwriting of the explanation of the emblem is not that of Gauden, but is in the style of a schoolmaster, which Dugard was. 6th, The blunder of Gauden himself about the Greek motto below the verses referring to Constantine instead of Constantius in his sermon on the 30th January, 1649/50, wherein he distinctly assigns the book to Charles I. 7th, The comparison of the sentences written by the King's own hand in his copy of Bacon's *Advancement of Learning* (a book which Gauden could never have seen until *after* Charles's death) with the style and method of composition of the *Eikon* itself.

Now to turn to the external evidence that has come to

light during the fifty years that have elapsed since Dr. Wordsworth gave to the world the result of his laborious research into this subject. One of the most valuable testimonies to the existence of a "Naseby copy" (*i.e.* a copy of the first seven chapters of the *Eikon*, which is said to have been taken by the Parliamentary forces, along with the Royal papers after the battle of Naseby), has lately turned up in the library at Lambeth Palace, where is preserved the copy of this work, formerly in the possession of Archbishop Tenison. On the last page in the Autograph of the owner is the following Memorandum.

"D[octor] Mew, L[ord] B[ishop] of Winchester, had often told me (& he repeated it again before ye B[ishop] of Peterburgh in ye B[isho]ps Cha[m]ber on Jan. 30th, 169⅔, bef[ore] we went to West[minster] Abbey, that at Naseby-fight he saw ye K[ing]s Closet Keeper before ye fight began carry out the Kings papers to ye Camp ; & y^t aft[e]r ye Fight he saw divers of them torn, & amo[n]gst these fragm[en]ts took up some pieces of εἰκ[ὼν] βασ[ιλικὴ] written with ye Kings own hand

Tho[mas] Cantuar[iensis]."

The existence of this Naseby copy has always been considered to be fatal to Gauden's claim, as he declared that he began to compose the *Eikon* in or about the year 1647, and all his supporters are unanimous in saying that the only papers lost by the King at Naseby were those published by the Parliament, and among these is no trace of the *Eikon*. Many of the arguments are based on the fact that no mention is found of *Eikon Basilike* in any books or correspondence previous to the King's death; but this is manifestly absurd, because the work only received its Greek title at the time of its publication. Dr. Wordsworth produced no less than nine evidences in favour of a Naseby copy, but taken collectively they are not so weighty or decisive as this newly-found Memorandum. It is very strange that Todd, who was Librarian at Lambeth Palace, should have mentioned two copies of the book as being in the library, and yet should have said nothing of Archbishop Tenison's copy, however damaging to the cause he was seeking to uphold. As however the edition is not an English one, but the Latin translation by Bishop Earle, he may have overlooked it altogether. One argument against the chronological arrangement of the *Eikon* is that events occur in chapters subsequent to the time at which they were apparently composed, and it has been answered that such circumstance is to be explained by the habit of the King to correct and retouch the part already written. But Bishop Mew furnishes us with another and better reason, viz., that the first seven chapters were so injured at the battle of Naseby, that the King must have rewritten them from the recovered fragments, and would naturally have added and altered many passages. Some considerable evidence, hitherto unknown, has also been found among the papers and official correspondence of Sir Edward Nicholas, Secretary of State to Charles I. and Charles II., which have been lately acquired by the British Museum. He was one of the most confidential servants of the former monarch, and their ciphered correspondence was published by W. Bray in 1818, in his Evelyn Memoirs from the originals in the Evelyn library at Wotton. Half, however, of the letters had never found their way to Wotton, but had remained at West Horseley, in Surrey, the ancient seat of the Nicholas family, and among them are six papers relating to the *Eikon*, a seventh having been found by Bray, at Wotton; and an eighth of the same series having been published by Wagstaffe in his *Vindication of King Charles the Martyr*. It will be necessary for the better understanding of the allusions in the new correspondence to first give a copy of the letter at Wotton, which is slightly earlier than the others.

Paris, Nov. 6, 1649, St. No.

SIR,

To giue you an account of the vastnesse of this Packett, give me leaue to tell you that together with this booke which I send you there came in half a score persons of consideration, who with very much passion, desired me to represent to Jersey the high indignity by this base edition offered to our blessed Master, and the great injury rendered to his Majesty that now is.

You will finde a Preface to this Booke which tends to proue that our blessed Master might be, nay, perhaps was a Papist in his heart, notwithstanding this Booke. That what instructions and commands were giuen to his sonne for his firmenesse to the Protestant Religion, were giuen out of politique considerations meerely, and many other particulars which I hope will bring it to the hands of the common hangman.

This Marsys is one who setting out the tryall of the late King, and the manner of his murther stiles himselfe "Interprete et Maistre pour la langue Francoise du Roy d'Angleterre regnant a present et de son Altesse Royale le Duc d'Yorke son frere" in which Booke he stiles Queene Elizabeth (of euer blessed memory) Jezabell. He sets downe a false and faigned speech of the Kings at the time of his being murthered; & being charged with it, he said he thought fitt to make that speech as spoken by him since the speech he did make was poore and belowe a King. He hath sett forth diuers other things, an extract whereof I shall shortly send you, the least of which would deserue a whipping in England in good times to speake moderately. I presume you will giue this business a thorough sifting there in Councell, and send some directions to Sir Richard Browne how to proceede here. That it may appeare who sett him on worke here, and who giues him these exact coppies which he pretends to haue under the Kings owne hand. And those other peeces of the Kings which he so braggs of, and promises he will bring them to light, so soone as he obtaines leaue to publish them. I hope some course wilbe taken that he may be discharged of his titles of relation to the King, and that his Majesty will hereupon giue order that a true coppy may be printed in French of his Fathers Booke, declared by him to be authentique, waving both the editions either of Huguenot or Papist, and that this command be grounded upon the ill Editions of both these Persons and Partys.

Indorsed "6° Novem : 1649. Concerning Marseis, his translacion of the Kings Booke."

This letter, as printed by Bray, has no signature to it, which has led him to propound a false conjecture as to the writer of it in his note upon its contents. He says, "If it were necessary to enter upon the controversy respecting the authenticity of *Eikon Basilike*, this letter might be adduced as a proof against Bishop Gauden's claim to that work. The wish here expressed was not fulfilled specifically ; though afterwards in some measure gratified by the publication of *Eikon Aklastos* in 1651, as a vindication of the original work against the attacks of Eikonoklastes. This letter," he goes on, " was written by Sir Edward Nicholas during his retreat from England after the death of his royal master. He appears to have been then resident with his son-in-law, Sir Richard Browne, who still remained chargé d'affaires at the French Court." This, of course, is an absurd mistake ; the letter in question being not *from* but *to* Nicholas, who was then at Jersey with Charles II. If Bray thought this letter might be adduced as a proof against Gauden's claim, what would he have said had he afterwards discovered the subsequent letter with its two enclosures, which was the direct result of this anonymous appeal. Between the date of the first letter on 6 November, 1649, and the date of the earliest newly discovered one on 4th January, 1650, there appears to have been a letter of the $\frac{13}{23}$ November from Nicholas, written in consequence of the first communication and addressed to Sir Christopher

Hatton, Sir Richard Browne, John Cosin, Dean of Peterborough, and George Morley afterwards Bishop of Winchester, all at this time resident at Paris. This letter apparently has not survived to the present day, or else it is hidden in the private papers of some old family, and will come to light at a future time. Its loss is much to be regretted, as it must have materially strengthened the evidence for Charles I. In consequence of this letter, Sir C. Hatton, Sir R. Browne, Dean Cosin and Morley seem to have sought an interview with Marsys, and which he avoided, until on 4th January, 1650, they are able to announce to Nicholas that they have at last succeeded in speaking with Monsieur Marsys, and they give a lengthy but extremely interesting and valuable account of their proceedings. We learn from their letter that so great was the demand for a French Edition of the *Eikon*, that four thousand copies of a translation by a Monsieur Porrée were already sold within twelve months after the King's death. In the instructions to Sir R. Browne (the draft of which the writers of the letter forward to Nicholas for the Royal approval and signature), Charles II. is made to declare in most distinct and precise words, his belief in his father being the author of the *Eikon*, and one or two words have been added to or corrected in the draft in Nicholas' own hand, proving thereby that it was taken into consideration and acted upon. These additional words are here printed in italics, to draw the reader's attention to them. The second enclosure is also curious and very interesting, especially the remark that Queen Henrietta Maria flung away Marsy's *Histoire de la Persecution presente des Catholiques d'Angleterre* near the time of the first edition on account of the false and slanderous passages against her honour in his Epistle dedicatory unto her. The following is the letter with its two enclosures :

SIR,

In obedience to his Maties Commands signified vnto us in yours of the 13/23 Novr wee haue at last spoken with Monsr Marsys (after some delayes on his Part) To whome wee represented his Maties Just sense and Indignation against the Preface, Title Page, References, and notes annexed to his Translation and Edition of the Booke written by his late Matie of euer blessed Memory.

Wee asked him upon what grounds, and by whose incouragement, priuity, or advice he presumed to put forth the Advertisement, Preface, and Notes upon that Translation, so boldly and scandalously insinuating that his late Matie was enclining to Popery.

To which he answered that as he had not been put upon this Worke by any, so had not any person been made aquainted therewith by him before the Impression of his Booke; but that upon generall Conference with those Protestants, and Roman Catholiques, with whome he had conversed, it was thought more advantagious to represent the late King a Roman Catholique then a Puritan as they conceiued Porrée had done, in regard, that it might be a meanes to stirre up the Romish Partie to helpe, and assist his Matie that now is; which would be of greater Concernement then any thing the Calvinists or Huguenotts would doe. He further added, That at his first vndertaking he had no intention to Prefixe any Preface, or adde any notes to his Edition, but that he was afterwards prouoked thereunto upon the Sight of Monsr Porrées Preface and wilfull Faults in his Translation.

Wee demanded of him; First, why he called the Booke intituled Le Portraict du Roy vn liure Aposté et Diffamatoire, which wee and all others (but himselfe) conceiued To be the Right and true translation of $εἰκὼν βασιλική$ the same being the Title affixed to that Booke when it was first printed in England, and therein translated. The Portraiture of his Sacred Matie as it was likewise rendred Imago Regis Caroli in the Latin Edition set forth in Holland, by the Approbation of his Matie that now is, Marsys himselfe hauing no other Copie to translate by, then those Two that had the same Title, which he calls Aposté, &c. And secondly being demanded, why he had not Suppress'd his new Imposed Title, together with his slanderous and bold assertion concerning the Former, which he might haue timely done upon the early Admonition of Sir Richard Browne, giuen him the day after the Titles of his Booke were first affixed to the publique Places of this Cittie, and before any of the Copies were deliuered out at the Printing-house, it being then likewise represented vnto him that in his new Title Page, He did not Charge the Booke entituled le Portrait du Roy &c. to be an ill Translated Booke but a meere Supposititious Booke, and that advantage would from hence be taken, in England, to increase, if not Confirme their Scandalls who gaue it out that εἰκὼν βασιλικὴ was not written by the late King; wherein his boldnesse had been also the greater, in that he had so excessiuely vilified that Edition, which he knew his Matie that now is by his Gracious Expressions, in his Royal Letters to Monsr Porrée had well accepted of, in regard both of his Paines and his early readinesse to render that excellent Booke vnto his owne nation in their owne Tongue, although through haste and want of a perfect vnderstanding in the English Tongue some errours and faultes might escape him in that Translation.

His answer to all this was, First, that Porrée had not truly translated the Title of εἰκὼν βασιλικὴ because to Portrait du Roy he had added these words De la Grand' Bretaigne and that thereupon he tooke his advantage to condemne the Booke that bare the Title of Portrait du Roy de la Grand Bretaigne. Secondly he said That (notwithstanding the aforesaid Admonition) the prevailing reason with him, not to suppresse or alter the Title of his Booke, was, because he thought he should haue lost much by it, if he had so done, his primarie Intention being, by this alteration of the Title, to make his owne Edition more vendible and hinder the Sale of Porrées, adding that it repented him he had not done it sooner, in regard there were foure thousand of Porrées Copies already disperst; and that those, with whome he convers'd, advised him to goe on, with his former designe, notwithstanding Sr Richard Browne's Admonition.

Being by us demanded, by what Authority he assumed to himselfe, in the Title Page before some of his Printed Bookes, the Style of Interprete & Maistre pour la langue Françoise du Roy d'Angleterre regnant a present et de son Altesse Royal Monseigneur le Duc d'Yorke son frere. He answered he did assume to himselfe that Title by reason he had the Hon^r to read French to his Matie that now is, when he was Prince of Wales, and was also assigned to the same Employment towards his Highnesse the Duke of Yorke.

Whilst we were in the prosecution of this Businesse, my Lord Bishop of Galloway (who accidentaly came in upon a Visit) desyred he might lay it to Marsys Charge, the wronge and Scandall he had done to the Royall Partie of the Scotts by applying to the Whole Nation what the King in the Beginning of the 23 Chapter of his Booke restraines onely to Those that deliuered him up: And he accused Marsys to be an unfaithfull Translator, in positiuely rendring what the King suppositiuely speakes. For whereas in the English the Kings words are Those Scotts and the Latin hath it right Istos Scotos and Monsr Porrée truly renders it Ces Escossois, Marsys makes it indefinite Escossois and whereas the King saith, If I am sold, wherevnto the Latin Translation agreeth expressing it Si ab ijs Divendar and Monsr Porrée likewise truly renders it Si je suis vendu, And although all the Kings loyall Scotch Partie, and amongst them my Lord Byshop himselfe (as he saith) might and doe belieue in their Perticular Judgements, that the King was Sold by that partie of Scotts which deliuered Him up. Yet Monsr Marsys had he been a faithfull Translator of the Kings owne words, ought not to haue taken upon him the Libertie to leaue out those Limitations and Conditions wherewith it pleased his Matie to expresse himselfe and by his vnfaithfull Translation render his Maties expressions to importe that the whole Scottish nation was guilty of having absolutely sold their King. Wherevnto Monsr Marsys (acknowledging that he had for this already been by some Scotchmen publiquely challenged and Questioned in the Streets and threaten'd with Blowes, and indeed not being able to Justifie the Fidelity of his Translation of which he had so much boasted, both in his Preface and elsewhere) answered, that He had already resolued to make an Apology for himselfe in that particular onely which he intended to Publish in Print.

We held it not amisse to Charge him further with some of those great Insolencies he hath Committed in all other the Bookes published in his Name, in particular, That in his Booke intituled A Narration of the Tryal and Murder of the late King (in which he had giuen himselfe the Title of Interprete & Maistre de la langue &c.) he calleth Queen Elisabeth an Impious Jezabell with other base expressions concerning Her, And taketh his liberty not onely to alter and omitt many parts of his Maties Speech vsed at the tyme of his Murder of purpose leauing out those pious expressions which testifyed to the world in what Religion that blessed and Royall Martyr dyed; but likewise to adde of his owne feigning what he thought fitt; and to represent his Sacred Matie as then expressing himselfe in such Language and Passion whereof the very Rebells and Murderers themselues neuer accused him.

In his Booke intituled Histoire de la Persecution presente des Catholiques d'Angleterre (to which he makes his Marginall Renvoys throughout all the Kings Booke) wee shewed him what vnfitt and scurrilous Language he had vttered of King James of euer blessed Memory, Grandfather to our Soueraigne that now is and of other his Royall Predecessours &c. (some particulars whereof are lined out in the Booke which wee now send) together with many other Passages concerning the Protestants of the Church of England, and the publique Lawes of that Kingdome, very Scandalous to be read and full of Falsehood.

To all which he answered, That he held himselfe obliged so to speake as he had done of Queen Elisabeth, King James &c. as he was a Roman Catholique and that what he had sayd of Protestants referred to the tymes of Queen Elisabeth and King James in which all the Protestants were of that Temper wherein he represented them, which Answer we conceiue to be a great Aggrauation of his Offence by extending those his false and Scandalous expressions to all the Members of the Church of England who liued or dyed during the Reignes of those two famous Princes.

And whereas we are commanded to vse our best endeauours to make stay of the Publishing of the said Translation and Preface; Wee beseech you to represent to his Maties Consideration, That it cannot be expected wee should obteine the Fauour of the State here to Suppresse this Booke euen for that very Reason for which wee would suppresse it, which is the Dresse he hath giuen it to fitt the Popish Interest; and if this might haue been hoped it had not been now to be acted, as it hath not been vnconsidered. But there are already so many Copies dispersed that to efface this malitious Scandall Some other course must be taken.

Hauing thus sent you this Accompt of the matter of Fact to the end you may informe his Matie of our Proceedings herein; wee shall in the next place obey his Maties Commands to certifie what vpon Consideration of the whole Businesse we humbly Conceiue fit to be done in it.

We therefore humbly offer as the onely expedient in our Judgement, upon the daily experience of the mischeivous Consequences both here and in England of these Insolencyes of Marsys; That his Matie will be pleased with the advice of his Councell to put in execution what this Inclosed Letter doth purport, and send the same Vnder his Royall Signet conteyning his commands and Directions in this Businesse vnto Sr Richard Browne as his Resident and Publique Minister in this Place, which letter wee haue drawne up in obedience to his Maties Commands, signified vnto us by one of yours of a late date.

And this we humbly conceiue to be the onely way now left to repaire the Injuries done by this Marsys and sufficiently to Righte his Matie in his Pious vindication, not onely of his blessed Father but likewise of his other Royall Predecessours, and Progenitors, together with his own Religious, Pious, and Royall Disposition and Intention.

Which we humbly beseech you to present to his Matie as a Testimony of our Obedience to his Commands and a

Pledge of our Zeale to the euer blessed Memory of our late Royal and blessed Master.

And so wishing you all health and
Happinesse we Remaine
            S^r
      Your most humble Servants

Paris 4th January.
Anno. 1650. s°. n°.

          Chr: Hatton.   Richard Browne.
          Jo: Cosin.   Geor: Morley.

"Right" Trusty and Welbeloued,—Whereas wee haue been informed by diuers Persons (uppon their obseruation of the publishing and vttering so large a Proportion of that Booke, which was written by our Father of euer blessed Memory, and entituled εἰκὼν βασιλική) hauing now passed three Impressions in the French Tongue in Rouen and Paris) That the said Booke is very acceptable vnto the French Nation and much approued and Desired by them in Generall; To the end that Right may be done to the said Booke and satisfaction to all such who justly esteeme and Value it, we haue thought it agreable to the great Regard and tender Affection wee beare to the Memory and Honour of our most dear and blessed ffather and to the Right Information of all those who desire to read and make vse of the Truth wisedome and Piety which is Conteyned in that Booke to take into our Consideration the Seuerall Translations already made thereof into the French tongue wherein wee find that of Monsieur Porrées entituled le Portrait du Roy de la Grand Bretaigne (being a True expression of the Title of our late Fathers Booke) first Printed at Rouen to haue *had* some mistakings, "and Errours" in it, which (as we belieue) escaped him, through haste, and for want of a perfect vnderstanding of the English Tongue, although wee doubt not but his meaning and Intentions were good which wee haue accordingly accepted from him; But whereas there is another pretended Translation, and Edition, set forth by one of that Nation calling himselfe, Le Sieur de Marsys to which he feigns a Title of his owne Invention as followeth; les Memoires du feu Roy de la Grand Bretaigne Charles premier escrits de sa propre main dans sa prison. Ou il est monstre que le liure intitulé Portrait du Roy de la Grand Bretaigne est vn liure Aposté et diffamatoire. Traduits de l'Anglois en nostre Langue par le Sieur du Marsys & enrichis d'Annotations & de Renuois tres necessaires pour l'Inteligence de l'Ouurage.

Wee haue seriously considered thereof and forasmuch as wee find that the said Marsys hath not onely boldly altered the True Title of our Deare Fathers Booke (which being stiled εἰκων βασιλικὴ is not vnproperly translated by Monsieur Porrée le Portrait du Roy de la Grand Bretagne) but likewise insolently averred in his owne New Title Page that the former Booke intituled (as it ought to be) is A Suposititious "Booke" and defamatory Booke, meerely out of an vnworthy designe by his owne Confession to hinder the Sale of Monsieur Porrées Edition, and to deceiue the Buyers by making them belieue that this Edition of his is a new distinct Booke from that sett forth by Monsieur Porrée; And further that the said Marsys hath annexed to the said Booke an Advertisement wherein are many things Scandalous to the Royall Person and Honour of our late ffather; and that he hath been likewise vnfaithfull in his Translation of some particulars, and amongst others of that which concerneth the Scotts whereby he hath cast an Infamy upon the whole Scottish Nation; and hath moreouer added many malitious Annotations together with diuers Renuois to an Insolent Booke formerly printed by him wee haue therefore thought fitt to declare our just Indignation against this his Edition, and to disclaime it.

And whereas this Marsys hath in another Booke intituled a Narration of the Tryall and Murder of the late King (our deare and blessed ffather) taken his licentious liberty to stile himselfe Interprete & Maistre pour la langue Françoise du Roy d'Angleterre Regnant a present et de son Altesse Royale Monseigneur le Duc d'Yorke (which wee neuer allowed him) and in the same Booke not onely with false and vnseemely Language to abuse the Person of Queen Elisabeth of Blessed Memory, but to injure also our Deare and blessed ffather by altering the Speech which at the time of his Murther and Martyredome he vttered to the People, therein leauing out particulars of greatest moment Concerning his Honour and representing him with such Language and passion as was much different from that Matie and Christian Piety wherewith he vnderwent that his Cruel and barbarous Martyredome and whereas a third Booke sett forth vnder the said Marsys name hath likewise come to our View intituled Histoire de la Persecution present des Catholiques d'Angleterre, &c.; wherein besides his insolent and malitious Aspersions cast upon other of our Predecessours in the Crowne of England he hath likewise with very false, and Scandalous language abused the Person, and Actions of our most deare Grandfather King James of euer blessed Memory, and throughout the greater part of that whole Booke hath shewed little else but his owne Boldnesse and Ignorance. Therefore (all these foregoeing Particulars Considered) wee haue by the advice of our Councell caused the two last forementioned Bookes set forth in the said Marsys name, together withe the Title Advertisement Notes and Renvoys of the other Booke entituled Les Memoires &c. *being stiled from our fathers said Booke* to be publiquely burnt in our Isle of Jersey by the Hande of the Common Hangman. And wee doe disavow the said Marsys to haue any Relation to our Service enioyning you to discharge him from assuming to himselfe any title of dependance upon us or our Brother the Duke of Yorke. And to the end that so Inestimable a Jewell as our Fathers Booke is may be rendred to that Nation where you Reside for us, and who entertaine it with due value and esteeme as neere the Pure originall Lustre as may bee, wee haue thought fitt to giue order for a Translation and an Edition thereof to be prepared and Set forth by Mons' Testard one of the Pastors of Bloys, an able learned man and well affected both to our blessed ffathers Honour and ours, and to the welfare of the Church of England. The Care in procureing whereof according to the True originall Copie wee haue Committed vnto our Chaplain D' Cosin Deane of Peterborough. Our Will and Pleasure therefore is that you our said Resident shall as our publique Ministre take Notice hereof and upon all fitting occasions and opportunityes according to your iudgement and discretion shall divulge and Publish as well the Censures wee haue executed upon the said Bookes of Marsys as likewise our auowing and approuing of this Edition of Monsieur Testards Translation; wherein you shall giue *your* assistance to further and Promote it in our name and Interests, and upon all occasions shew such Respect and Kindnesse to the said Mons' Testarde and any other whome he shall employ for the Publishing thereof as may agree with his and their Juste desires, or your carefull and Reasonable performance; And for so doing this shall be your warrant. Giuen vnder our   at Castle Elizabeth In our Island of Jersey.

To our Trusty and Welbeloued
S' Richard Browne Kn' &
Baronet Our Resid'.

Scandalous Passages false Traductions
and Contradictions in Marsys Booke
styled Les Memoires &c.;

In the Kings Portraiture

He takes away the Crowne of Glory which was in the English and Latin Copie.

In his Title Page.

1. The Change of the True Title of the Booke first printed in England and after in Holland in English and Latin.

2. His averring in his Title Page that the Booke Intituled Portrait du Roy &c. is a Counterfeit and supposititious Booke.

3. His Boldnesse in making many impertinent and diuers malitious Annotations upon his Maties Booke and therein adding Renuoys vnto a Scandalous Booke formerly set forth vnder his the said Marsys name

In his Preface

He takes upon him to tell the world that the king made no title to his Chapters in the Originall Booke which is more then he could say truly, for by his owne Confession he had not the sight of any other Copie but what was set forth in English and Latin where those titles of Chapters were printed in the third Person which as a Translator he ought to haue followed.

In the Advertisement.

1. In the fourth Page his falsehood in averring Que le Roy en d'autres endroits ne se sert pas de ce Terme (Papistes) mais de celuy de Catholique Romain, whereas the

King throughout his whole Booke giues them no other Appellation but that of Papists.

2. Ibidem. Another false Assertion in saying that the Church of England hath retayned the same order and the same gouernment with that Catholique Church which euerywhere in his Bookes (as he confessed in his Conference with us) he understands to be the Roman Church.

3. Ibidem. A third false Assertion that there is no Community or Resemblance either in doctrine or in Gouernment between the Protestants of England and those whome he Calls Calvinists.

4. Ibidem. A fourth fal[s]e Assertion that of a good Protestant they may as easily make a (Roman) Catholique as a Riseing Sunne of a faire Morning.

5. A Calumnie upon the blessed king where raising to himselfe an objection that some perhaps will say the King paroist Protestant he answereth that though he had not been a Protestant it concerned him to write as he hath done for reason of State to take away the Accusation of those that said he was a (Roman) Catholique in his heart whereby Marsys doth not onely attempt to make it doubtfull of what Religion the King was, but to Render him also a most notorious Hypocrite in his life and death.

6. Another, that where the king exhorts his Sonne to be firme in the Protestante Religion it may be belieued it was for feare onely he should be Come a Calviniste whereas it is euident that the king mentioneth no Calvinist in that whole Chapter but exhorts him from the Pompe of that superstitious Tyrannie (and whome that meant Marsys knew well enough) and from the meanes of Fantasticke Anarchie whome all the world knowes to bee "whome all the world knowes" ye new Anabaptisticall Sects.

7. Another Calumny Que le Roy ne Choque Jamais les Catholiques (Romains) que pour Reiller les Heretiques (Calvinistes).

8. Where he makes an apologie for the late horrid Rebellion in Irelande, with these words Quelle Religion n'a point ceste Maxime de Chercher la liberté de Conscience as if it were lawfull to seeke the same (as they did) by Rebellion.

9. A sawcy Contradiction giuen to the king by a petulant Retortion of his Maties owne words in saying that les

Irelandois font bien voir a present que les Catholiques (Romains) ont des maximes qui authorisent moins la Rebellion, que celles des Heretiques.

10. He sayth that the Popish Irish sont les seuls sujets des Isles Britanniques qui soient a present fideles à leur Roy by which impudent assertion he excludes from all fidelity to the king not onely the Marquis of Ormond and all other Protestants with in his Army and Guarisons in Ireland, but likewise all and euery other his Maties Protestant Subjetts whomesoeuer in England and Scotland together with the Isles of Man and Jersey (which are as Britannique as Ireland) thereby numbring them all among the Rebells and Traitors to the King.

11. That the kings Booke is so full of Invectiues against the Calvinistes as if he had Composed his Booke to Confound them onely whereas the King in all his Booke nameth them not.

12. Pretending to Recite the Kings words concerning Churchwindowes, Crosses and Inscriptions upon the Monuments of the Dead, he repeats them vntruly and inferres from them the kings defence of Popery and Superstition which is cleane differente from the expresse Termes and Sense of his Maties Booke.

13. He reproues the Translator of Rouen for hauing an ill designe, because he sought not his Maties leaue to Translate the Booke nor Communicated his Traduction to the English at Rouen before he printed it, whereby he makes an argument against himselfe of his owne ill designe, who by his owne Confession (to us) was guilty of both these faults, which he blames in Monsr Porrée.

14. The Sentence that Marsys giues of Monsieur Porrées booke is, Ceux qui ont ce liure diffamatoire sont obliges d'Inuiter Plusieurs Personnes d'honneur et de tendre Conscience qui l'ont mis au feu and when his Title Page, Advertisement, Annotations, and Translations are well perused this will appeare a good Paterne for a Censure upon his workes.

15. That which the King calls Inscriptions of the Dead (as Marsys himselfe reads it in his Translation of that Place) is in this Advertisement out of opposition to Porrée translated Epitaphs des Catholiques (Romains).

16. Vndertaking to proue that the Booke called Portrait du Roy is Counterfeit he acknowledgeth that both it and that of his owne are taken from one and the same Originall, and yet that one of them (meaning Porrées) is not the Kings.

17. He pretends to haue seen the kings manuscript and from thence inferres that the additionall Peices concerning the Discourse of the King to his Childeren, the Duke of Glocester and the Princesse Elizabeth are malitiously annexed to the Second Edition of Porrées Translation, who therein followed the Copie Imprinted in England giuen vnder that Princesse owne hand, which this Marsys Sawcily Sensureth to be partiall and absurd, as well for the Kings Recommendation of the Bookes there named to her, as for her Incapacity to vnderstand the smallest Rudiments of Christianity.

18. He is too bold to owne and Publish to the world his knowledge or sight of another Booke Composed by the King which himselfe Confesseth for Certaine Reasons is not yet to be set forth, but insinuateth that hereafter he shall be the man who shall set it forth.

In a short view that we tooke of his Translation wherein he boasteth to haue been so religeously exact that he hath not altered nor taken away one Iota we find as followeth.

Chap. 1. he translateth the words other Gentlemen la plus Part des Membres;

Ibidem. Whereas the King saith—the Health of all States and kingdomes *Marsys saith* States onely and leaues out kingdomes.

Chap. 7, parag. 8. Impudence is translated D'Imprudence.

Ibidem. The Kings words—Wee doe not much blame the vnkindnesse of the generality & vulgar, Marsys translateth Puisque nous Cognoissons que le general en est Innocent.

Ibidem. to the Kings words—of eating our bread headds —Comme on dit.

Chap. 8. Parag. 10 being Compared with the Kings booke, Marsys Translation appeareth to be very defectiue.

Chap. 12. Whereas the King saith—By how much protestant Principles are more against all Rebellion against Princes then those of Papists. Marsys rendereth these words—Que les Principes des Protestants asseurent plus les Monarques contre la Rebellion que Ceux des Papistes. Wherein he Committeth the same fault that in his advertisement he blameth in Porrée for not observing the literall Translation of this particular Place.

Chap. 15. The King vseth foure tymes the wordes papists, and Marsys thrice translateth it Catholique Romain; of which distinction framed onely by himselfe he maketh a vaine and false vse, in his advertisement against Porrée, and to make good this his feigned difference doth in one and the same paragraph of this Chapter render the word Papists by the Terme of Romane Catholique in the first part thereof and Papist in the latter.

Chap. 23. Where the King restraines his words to those Scotts, that deliuered him up, Marsys enlargeth his translation to Escossois in generall. And where the King saith, If I am sold which is conditionall Marsys turnes it absolutely, le Regret que i'ay d'estre vendu.

In his Annotations and Renvois.

Page 2. Where the kinge speaketh of his interest in Religion, Marsys saith it is because he tooke upon him the Title of Head in Spirituall Matters against which (though the King neuer tooke that title) he inveigheth in his Booke, whereunto he referreth.

Pag. 35. Where the king Speaketh of his prayers and Teares, Marsys addeth his Note, that they were vnprofitable, if they came not from the heart.

Pag. 38. Where the King referreth to himselfe in naming the Restored Glory of the Suns height after his Ecclypse Marsys noteth it in his Margent for a Clinch saying SVN Qui signifie Soleil en Anglois signifie aussi fils ; le Roy par cette Equivoque touche elegament le Restablissement du Roy d'a present son fils.

Page 39. He makes his boldnesse and sayth It seemeth the King foresaw that God could not saue him without a Miracle.

Page 47. At the Kings word Papist Marsys noteth, that the King doth not say Catholiques, and yet in his Advertisement he plainely saith that he did vse this word here, and Referres to this very place.

Page 48. The Kings Words against the Irish Rebells—
Ce peuple estant desia assez disposé a des violences exorbitantes, tant per quelques maximes de leur Religion &c.
Marsys to excuse them noteth La Reyne Elizabeth a fort
persecutè les Irelandois. And upon the words Maximes—
De repouster la force, Qui vous Constraint dans vostre
Religion, cette Maxime est commune a toute Sorte de
Religions. A bold and a false note (especially upon the
Kings words) and againe les Irelandois se resouuenent des
cruautes que les Protestants auoient exerces sur eux se
vangerent par cette occasion, qu'ils entrouerent. As if this
were a just excuse for their rebellion.

Page 78. Vpon the Kings words, l'orgueil de quelque
gens, Marsys makes this note Luther and Calvin & les
Autres Princes et estats qui ont embrassé leur nouuelle
doctrine, As if the Kings expression had Reference to them.

Page 122. Where the King expresseth himselfe cleerely
as in many other places in his Booke for his Sonnes
Constancy in the Protestant Religion of the Church of
England Marsys noteth in his margin, Il entend la Religion
Chrestienne en general.

In Monsieur Marsys his Histoire de la Persecution
presente &c.

There will be found in those seuerall Places wee haue scored
with red Inke many false and slanderous Passages.

1. Against the Realme of England.
2. Against the honour of the Queen of Great Bretagne in his Epistle dedicatory vnto her for which she flung it away nere the tyme of the First Edition.
3. Against King Henry the 8th.
4. Against Queen Elizabeth.
5. Against King James.
6. Against King Charles.
7. Against the lawes of England.
8. Against the Judges of England.
9. Against the Church of England.

In his Processe Concerning the Kings Death.

1. Marsys vndertaking (in his litle [Title] Page) to translate the English Copie faithfully which he performeth not.
2. Au Lecteur. He pretends that the Kings Ennemies

sett forth that Relation in English, and that ye Translation of Rouen followed a false Copie yet Marsys himselfe had no other.

3. He giues notice to the world of his Booke (called the Persecution of England) that it might be enquired after and sell the better.

4. Page the 8. He calls Queen Eliz:[abeth] an Impious Jezabell (which he found not in his Copie).

5. Pag. 9. He adds 24 lines of his owne head to abuse the kingdome and King Henry the 8.

6. Page 11 & 12. He alters all the Kings Speech omitts a great part of it, and makes his last words to be spoken in a disordered Passion Tenez Traistres.

7. Page 13 & 14. Of the fiue Paragraphs that follow, those are added of his owne head, who promised in his Title to be a faithfull Translatour.

A period of ten years now elapses in the Nicholas papers before any further allusion to the *Eikon* is to be found, but only ten days before Charles II. returns to take possession of his kingdom, he writes a brief note to Monsieur Porrée, who figures so often in the letter with its enclosures just given. In the note the King thanks Porrée for apparently a new French translation of the *Eikon*, which he still calls his Father's book. The letter is the original draft revised and corrected, and consequently does not bear the King's stamp or signature.

Breda, May 20, 1660.

MONSIEUR PORREE,

Jay tousjours souhaitte de voir le liure du feu roy Mon Pere en beau francois et vous auez touché mes souhaits cela et le soin que vous auez de desabuser le monde en ce qui est de la fermete de ma creance marque" nt " asses laffection que vous faites profession d'auoir pour moy et dont "jay tire" vous mauez donné beaucoup de preuues ; aussy vous puisje asseurer que j'en ay tout le ressentiment qu'il faut et comme je pretends de dementir par ma constance dans la religion "protestante" Reformee tous les faux bruits que mes ennemis ont malicieusement fait courir a mon "deso" preiudice "par ma constance dans la Relligion Protestante": vous deues croire que je noublieray pas les bons offices que vous me rendes en repoussant ces calomnies qui mattaquent par ou je suis le plus "le plus" sensible, et que je seray tousjours.

Endorsed "A MONSIEUR PORREE."

At the close of the same year 1660, on 29th November, Charles II. granted to Royston, the publisher (who had printed the first edition of the *Eikon*), the monopoly of printing his Father's works, and in the patent calls that book "the most excellent discourses and soliloquies of our blessed Father." Among the Nicholas papers is a printed broadside containing the original advertisement of this complete edition, which unhappily perished a few years later in the celebrated Fire of London. It runs thus—

"M.S.
Sanctissimi Regis, & Martyris, Caroli.
Siste Viator.
Luge, Obmutesce, Mirare!
Memento Caroli Illius
Nominis pariter, & Pietatis Insignissimæ, Primi
Magnæ Britanniæ Regis:
Qui Rebellium Perfidia primo Deceptus
Dein Perfidorum Rabie Percussus
Inconcussus tamen Legum & Fidei Defensor,
Schismaticorum Tyrannidi Succubuit.
Anno
Salutis Humanæ, MDCXLVIII.
Servitutis Nostræ, } Primo,
Fælicitatis Suæ,   }
Corona Terrestri Spoliatus, Cælesti Donatus.
Sileant Autem Perituræ Tabellæ.
Perlege Reliquias, ære Sacras, Carolinas,
In Queis
Sui Mnemosynem, œre perenniorem
vivacius exprimit
Illa, Illa,
ΕΙΚΩΝ ΒΑΣΙΛΙΚΗ.

"This is placed with his Majesties Pourtraicture in St. Olaves Silver Street Church, in London, with his Works in Folio under it."

Sir Edward Nicholas has left behind him a great many memoranda on various subjects, some political, some theological, &c.; written on backs of envelopes addressed to himself, or on any little scraps of paper he happened to have by him. These are in many cases exceedingly interesting and important, especially some autobiographical notes of his chequered career. But on the back of an envelope addressed to him while in exile, and on some blank sheets of letterpaper, are about a dozen pages of moral and religious maxims and apophthegms, borrowed chiefly from the Bible. Interspersed among them are three sentences selected from "the King's Book." They do not appear to have been copied from any printed edition of that work, as the reference is to folios, not pages. First he quotes from Chapter VIII. of the *Eikon*, "The excesse of impotent passions iniures a man more than his greatest enemies can. K[ing]es booke. 56." Secondly, from Chapter XI., "Tumults are the hounds that attend the cry and hollow of those men, who hunt after faccions and priuat designs to the ruyne of Church and State. K[ing]es booke. fol. 97." (This quotation from *fol.* not *page* 97, brings to remembrance that Nicholas Oudart, Secretary to Sir Edward Nicholas, is said to have transcribed the King's original manuscript for the press, and it is not at all unlikely that Sir E. Nicholas had this MS. copy by him while making these extracts from the *Eikon*.) Thirdly, from Chapter XII., "The goodness of mens intentions will not excuse the scandall and contagion of ill examples. K[ing]es booke. 105." Here in this quotation is a slight variation from the printed copies, which read "*their* examples," instead of "*ill* examples;" another proof that

Sir E. Nicholas was citing a manuscript, not a printed copy. These moral and religious memoranda were most likely written during his leisure moments, after his retirement from the Secretaryship of State, and therefore some years subsequent to the date of his letter to Gauden found among the North papers, which has been supposed by the Bishop's supporters to show Nicholas' knowledge of the true author of the *Eikon*. On none, however, of these papers of Sir E. Nicholas is there the slightest note or endorsement by him to show that he knew the opinions and sentiments expressed in them respecting the *Eikon* and Charles I. to be either mistaken or false, or that he had ever heard of or been made acquainted with Gauden's claim.

The only remaining document as yet unnoticed among the Nicholas papers is an English letter from John Earles, Chaplain to Charles II., in which he dedicates to him his Latin translation of the *Eikon*. It is undated, but must have been written about the summer of 1649. The Latin copy of this letter is printed before all the Latin editions of the *Eikon*, but the English one is slightly fuller, and being the original of the Latin, and apparently unpublished, may be useful in support of the King's cause.

To the Kings most sacred Majesty.

May it please your Matie.

To receive into your gratious protection this image and pourtraict of your glorious Father (wherein he is nearer the similitude of God then as he is either a man or king) which though it appeare in a forraigne dresse and colour, yet it is such, as will make it more visible, and by consequence more publicke; for so I understood your Majesties pleasure was, that it should be deliuered to the world in a language common to the most part of the world: wherein I heartily wish I could haue done your Maj^{ty} that satisfactory service, as to haue rendered it in that naturall elegancy, and cleere and liuely expressions, wherewith the admirall originall aboundeth; which as it may puzzle perhaps the best master of language, soe it is much too hard for me; And yet as it is, I conceiue it much better, that it should even thus discoloured, and with some blemish of its lustre and excellency, converse with the greatest part of Europe, then to be confined to a few of his owne nation, and be silent to all the world besides; since there are here (if I may speake it with reuerence) some of those great things of God, which it concernes mankind to be made publique in all languages.

I have endeavoured according to my small ability to render it, if not in the same beauty, yet with the greatest truth and perspicuity, being not willing to depart from the very phrase and stile, so farr as the different Idiome of ye Latin would permitt me; since of so sacred a booke, as this is, we ought to be religious interpreters. And truly next that most sacred booke (wch admitts of no comparisons) I hope it will be no boldnes to say, that never any meerely humane worke has deserued so much esteeme, either for ye author or the argument.

Certainly the piety of Royall Persons deriues something from the height of their condition and has somewhat more noble and divine and wch challenges a greater power over the soules of men, and is received with more reverence then those of inferior ranke and quallity, for which cause God himselfe has been pleased in those parts of Scripture, wch more particularly belong to his worship, and are of perpetuall vse in the Church (such as Psalmes and Himmes and Prayers are) to make Princes his Instruments in the composing and conveying them to the world, to adde the more authority & Majesty vnto them. Men generally take vp devotion with a much better appetite when it is thus offered and presented; As we see by experience in this very Booke, wch all that vnderstood it were very much affected with, and wil be euery day much more, when being put into more languages it shalbe more vnderstood.

A rare and admirable thing it was thus to meditate, thus to compose, but a thing of much more admiration to liue, and to dye so: that these great expressions of piety, wch may seeme too bigg for any mans thought, were outdone by this great example. This that vnhappy part of the world, the most sinfull at this day, and the most polluted, is too sad a wittnes of. Oh how well had it been for them if they had sooner vnderstood that excellent vertue which now too-too late they admire & deplore, since it hath past the tryall of that terrible fornace, the greatest calamity to vs, but to him the greatest blessednesse imaginable, even that last and saddest part of his life, and that fatall day (wherein he was made a spectacle to men and angells, and gave such excellent proofs of a strong faith, & most invincible courage and constancy standing above all his sufferings and all the malice of Hell heaped together) was beyound all the glories and tryumphs of earthly Princes. You have done nothing, O you of all mankind the ——! (but I will not speake any horrible word in the entrance of so holy a Booke, nor make them the object of my curse, that are so much a part of his prayers) you have done nothing I say in this murder, but only joyned his Glory and Immortality with your owne eternall shame and reproach! Never any King since the Creation was lamented with so many true teares, extolled with so hearty and vnfayned applauses. Never did any in his most flourishing condition, extort from the feare, or buy from the flattery of their subjects those false & lying commendations, as were freely paid to his afflictions, to his overthrowes, to his Prison, to his Scaffold, and that direfull & dismall Axe, wherewith he astonished his Enemys dying, and tryvmphed over his murderers.

In the meanetime I doubt not but your sacred Matie (who are the true & liuely Portraict of your Royall Father, whose greatest happinesse in his prosperity, & greatest comfort in adversity was, that he had such a sonne in whom he cannot dye) will take flame from this example, not to revenge his death only (to which it may become others to incite you rather than myselfe), but to imitate that Heroicall virtue and constancy, and to take possession of that (whereof no force can deprive you against your will) the Inheritance of Religion and Piety. And as you are of tender affections to all those that have neer Relations to you, so I hope you will be pleased to extend them in some measure to this Booke, a Child of the same Father.

"Prov: 7-4. Say vnto wisedome thou art my sister, and to vnderstanding thou art my kinswoman." Advise with it. Converse with it, and transfuse it into thy very soule and spiritt. You see the eyes of all men are cast vpon you, all the hopes of good men fixed in you, all their liues depending on you, which noe doubt many men had long since out of ye extremity of their calamitys abandoned, but that they reserved them meerely to imploy in your service. A great businesse attends you great expectation great difficultys and such as require a greater taske and proportion of virtue then was before in any of your Predecessors. Whether there shall be a Kingdome any more in Britanny, whether Religion, whether Men, whether God againe, depends meerely vpon your virtue, your fortune or rather your fortune vpon Gods mercy, of the necessity of whose present assistance as your Matie must needs be now much more sensible, so I doubt not but that you will labour to procure it by all the dutys of Piety and Religion, and that all these happy seedes (so abundantly shed in your Royall breast) of Justice, Temperance, Prudence, and Goodnesse, may be nourished heightened and ripened to perfection, that God at length appeased and wholly reconciled may be graciously pleased to add that to your Matie wch he tooke from your Father, & to recompence his sorrowes in redoubled blessings, that you may be called That Restorer, wch is the hope and desire of all, and the most earnest & fervent prayer of

  Your Maj^{tys}
   most humble and devoted
    Subject & Chaplaine,
     JOHN EARLES.

It is a curious fact that the writer of this letter succeeded Gauden in the bishopric of Worcester, and yet so far as is known he never uttered any opinions or left any writings to show that he altered in the slightest degree his belief so strongly expressed in his dedication of his Latin edition that Charles I. had composed the *Eikon*. To sum up, therefore, the new external evidence during the last fifty years in behalf of the Royal Author, we have—1st, The holograph memorandum of Archbishop Tenison in his copy of Earles' Latin translation now in the Lambeth Library, which completely establishes, on the evidence of a most credible eye-witness, the existence of a Naseby copy, a fact alone sufficient to extinguish utterly Gauden's story of his forgery. 2nd, The letter with its two enclosures from Sir C. Hatton, Sir R. Browne, Dean Cosin, and Morley, which alludes more than once to the King's original manuscript as if still in existence, and about to be entrusted to Dean Cosin's keeping. 3rd, The letter from Charles II. to Porrée ten years later, on the eve of his Restoration, in which he again terms the *Eikon* the book of the late King, his Father. 4th, The original broadside advertisement of the new edition of the work in December, 1660, published under Royal patronage by Royston (a month subsequent to Gauden's first appeal to Charles II.), wherein it is described at length as the work of Charles I. 5th, The three selections by Sir E. Nicholas *after* 1663 from the King's Book, where he evidently quotes not a printed book, but a Manuscript Copy. 6th, The English original of John Earles' Latin dedicatory letter of his translation.

In conclusion, to show how base a timeserver Bishop Gauden was, and how utterly unfit he was to concoct such a forgery, it will be necessary to reproduce an unpublished letter written by his own hand in the name of himself and his wife to Henry Cromwell, Lord Deputy of Ireland, the younger son of Oliver Cromwell, at that time Lord Protector. It occurs in the correspondence of Henry Cromwell, now preserved among the Lansdowne MSS. in the British Museum, No. 822, f. 1.

"My Lord the renowne of your Lordships gouerment with such piety justice and clemency as giues life and recouery to that state of Ireland which was lately languishing & dying This (just Honor) hath made many your Lordships admirers who (yet) are humbly obseruant of that distance wherein they stand to your Lordships eminent place and authority noe lesse than your virtues; In this number I may owne my selfe and my wife whose great content it is to heare of that happines which your Lordship and your Lady enjoy; and to find by that Gentleman who lately came from your Lordship that wee alsoe are soe happy as to reteine some place in your memorys and fauours of which he gaue vs soe particular assurance that wee haue taken this Confidence to expresse our thankfull sense of that honor your Lordship and your Lady are pleased to doe vs when you voutsafe to think a kind thought of vs as persons condemned to obscurity; never to bee releiued except by such a barren way of industry as is sometimes giuen mee by such sad occasions as that of my nephew Will Russells and Mr. Rob. Richs death. To the vrne of this last I haue beene invited by your Lordships Sister the Lady Frances to Consecrate a litle monument; which possibly may (as marble) bee durable though it bee fruitlesse; vnlesse it bee productive of your Lordships fauour and acceptance, beyond that degree which it expects in England; The fate of books is like that of many trees to bring forth nothing but leaues. Being not read by many and valewed by few especially yf they strike vpon just securitys becoming all good Christians and wise to lay to heart; Noe discouragements in England haue hindred mee from presenting my sense of otheres deathes & my owne mortality to your Lordships view. The rather because I haue heard that your Lordship hath beene a noble asserter of our Richs honor even in Ireland; The vindication of which I willingly vndertook against a great streame of vulgar credulity; Being satisfied in this that I did the part of justice & gratitude to the dead; My ambition must bee to performe such actions as are their owne reward; among which I hope this is one; a copy of which I adventure vpon your Lordships and your Ladys acceptance; who in your highest secular advancements carry soe moderate a temper of minde & actions as willingly reflects vpon the end of all these momentary dreams; It is some recompense to my paines that I haue hereby an opportunity to expresse to your Lordship & your excellent Lady how much wee are ambitious to live worthy of that fauour your Noblenesses were pleased to expresse to

Your Lordships very
Humble Servants,
JOHN ELIZABETH GAUDEN.

LONDON,
May 24,
1658."

The address on the back of the letter is—

"These
to the right Honourable
the Lord Deputy of
Ireland,
    present."

In another hand, probably that of Henry Cromwell, is the endorsement—

"24 May 58.
MR. JO. GAUDEN."

If this fulsome letter from Gauden and his wife to one of the chiefest men in that Commonwealth which had taken the place and usurped the functions of the supposed Royal author of the *Eikon* be compared with the Bishop's letters written within three years from this date to the Lord Chancellor Hyde and the Earl of Bristol, the comparison will prove at once profitable and suggestive. In his earlier letter he thus speaks of books: "The fate of books is like that of many trees, to bring forth nothing but leaves. Being not read by many and valued by few, especially if they strike upon just securities becoming all good Christians and wise to lay to heart." But in his later letter to Hyde, on 21st Jan., 1660-1: "When it (his book, the *Eikon*) came out, just upon the King's death, Good God! what shame, rage and despite filled his Murtherers! What Comfort his friends! How many enemies did it Convert! How many hearts did it mollify and melt! What devotions it raysed to hys posterity, as children of such a father! What preparations it made in all mens minds for this happy restauration, and which I hope shall not prove my affliction! In a word, it was an army, and did vanquish more than any sword could." Again, in his letter to H. Cromwell (the son of the chief of those men whom he calls in the passage just quoted the King's *Murtherers*), he writes: "We have taken this Confidence to express our thankful sense of that honour your Lordship and your Lady are pleased to doe us when you vouchsafe to think a kind thought of us, as persons condemned to obscurity." But in his letter to Lord Bristol, of the 20th March, 1661-2, he uses the same expression to the most influential person in the Court of the *murdered* King's son: "How much I have of gratitude and honour for you whose eminent lustre hath condescended to owne hym whom some men [*i.e.*, Clarendon and Morley] have banished to soe great an obscurity." One more quotation is sufficient. In his letter to H. Cromwell he says: "My ambition must bee to performe such actions as are their owne reward." In his letter to Lord Bristol, of 27th March, 1662, he tells us his actions during the Commonwealth were by no means of that nature, but that he was "Sufficiently knowne to all the English world by those many great and publique works I had done in my spheare to the hazard of my estate, liberty and life, in order to preserve and restore the just interests of the Church and Crown in the worst of times and things. Both enemies and friends saw me always standing in the gap with a bold and diligent loyalty, doing my duty by preaching, printing, and acting to the great vexation and confusion of those tyrants and usurpers." Among the chief of these tyrants and usurpers was Henry Cromwell, Lord Deputy of Ireland, his patron and friend only three years before. And yet this Gauden is the man whom, on his own unsupported testimony (for his wife and his curate, Dr. Walker, only derive their evidence and story second-hand from him), so many credulous persons, too indolent to inquire or examine for themselves, believe to have been the sole composer and author of the *Eikon Basilike*, a work which bears on every page the peculiar stamp of Charles's mind and habit of thought, and which betrays over and over again an intimate acquaintance with passing events to the minutest details, which could only have been known to the King. It were a fitting tribute to the memory of Bishop Gauden that the letter from himself and his wife should be written in letters of brass, and placed along with his effigy in Worcester Cathedral, to accompany the *Eikon Basilike* which he there holds in his hands, or at least that sentence of the letter which almost sounds prophetic of his own tomb: "A little monument, which possibly may, as marble, be durable, though it be fruitless."

EDWARD SCOTT.

30 Jan., 1880.

MR. EDWARD SCOTT *has much pleasure in announcing that, while the present sheets were passing through the press,* Mr. JOHN B. MARSH *has made the most valuable and interesting discovery in corroboration of the Royal Authorship that has yet fallen to the lot of any inquirer into the subject. He has found in the Record Office the original of the Second Prayer at the end of the* EIKON *(page* 224*), in the handwriting of Charles I., of the date* 1631, *and it contains a few trifling differences from the printed copy.—March* 22, 1880.

An article upon this discovery, setting forth in parallel columns the Prayer in the handwriting of the king and the version as it appeared in the first edition of the EIKON, *will appear in* THE ANTIQUARY *for May.*

Εἰκων Βασιλικὴ.

THE POURTRAICTURE
OF
HIS SACRED
MAJESTIE
IN
HIS SOLITUDES
AND
SUFFERINGS.

Rom. 8.
More then Conquerour, &c.

Bona agere, & mala pati, Regium est.

Reprinted
In R. M. *An. Dom.* 1 6 4 8.

CONTENTS.

———o———

	PAGE
I. Upon His Majesty's Calling this last Parliament	1
II. Upon the Earl of Strafford's Death	5
III. Upon His Majesty's going to the House of Commons	10
IV. Upon the Insolency of the Tumults	14
V. Upon His Majesty's Passing the Bill for the Triennial Parliaments, and, after settling this, during the Pleasure of the Two Houses	21
VI. Upon His Majesty's Retirement from Westminster	27
VII. Upon the Queen's Departure and Absence out of England	34
VIII. Upon His Majesty's Repulse at Hull, and the Fates of the Hothams	38
IX. Upon the Lifting and Raising Armies against the King	44
X. Upon their Seizing the King's Magazines, Forts, Navy, and Militia	54

		PAGE
XI.	Upon the Nineteen Propositions first sent to the King, and more afterwards	61
XII.	Upon the Rebellion and Troubles in Ireland .	73
XIII.	Upon the Calling in of the Scots, and their Coming	82
XIV.	Upon the Covenant	90
XV.	Upon the many Jealousies raised, and Scandals cast upon the King, to stir up the people against him . .	100
XVI.	Upon the Ordinance against the Common Prayer-book	113
XVII.	Of the Differences between the King and the Two Houses, in Point of Church Government . . .	121
XVIII.	Upon Uxbridge Treaty, and other Offers made to the King	137
XIX.	Upon the various Events of the War; Victories and Defeats	142
XX.	Upon the Reformation of the Times . .	149
XXI.	Upon His Majesty's Letters taken and divulged . .	156
XXII.	Upon His Majesty's leaving Oxford, and going to the Scots	162
XXIII.	Upon the Scots delivering the King to the English, and his Captivity at Holdenby	165
XXIV.	Upon their denying His Majesty the attendance of his Chaplains	169

PAGE

XXV. Penitential Meditations and Vows in the King's Solitude at Holdenby 180

XXVI. Upon the Army's Surprisal of the King at Holdenby, and the ensuing Distractions in the Two Houses, the Army, and the City 184

XXVII. To the Prince of Wales 191

XXVIII. Meditations upon Death, after the Votes of Non-Addresses, and His Majesty's closer Imprisonment in Carisbrook Castle 207

Private Prayers used by His Majesty in the time of his Sufferings 223

The Explanation of the EMBLEME.

mne mali, probris, gravat...	Though clogg'd with weights of miseries
ens, Palma ut Depressa, r...to.	Palm-like Depress'd, I higher rise.
n Fluctûs Ventiq; furent...	And as th' unmoved Rock out-bravo's
ipes immota repello.	The boistrous Windes and raging waves:
ris, cœlestis sidera, coru...	So triumph I. And shine more bright
n-felici pace triumpho	In sad Affliction's Darksom night.
rutilo gemmisq; micant...	That Splendid, but yet toilsom Crown
n spernendò calco Coronam.	Regardlosly I trample down
facilem, quo Spes mea, (hristi	With joie I take this Crown of thorn,
n est tractare molestum	Though sharp, yet easie to be born.
dei, semperq;-beatam	That heav'nlie Crown, already mine,
Specto, Nobisq; paratam.	I View with eies of Faith divine.
erno; quod Christi Gratia pr...t,	I slight vain things; and do embrace
Virtutis Gloria mer...	Glorie, the just reward of Grace.

Τῷ Χῷ δεῖ πάσχειν τῶν πόλιν, δεῖ τὸ Κάππα.

G.D.

EIKON BASILIKE.

I.

Upon His Majesty's Calling this last Parliament.

THIS last Parliament I called, not more by others' advice and necessity of my affairs than by my own choice and inclination, who have always thought the right way of Parliaments most safe for my crown, as best pleasing to my people. And although I was not forgetful of those sparks which some men's distempers formerly studied to kindle in Parliaments (which, by forbearing to convene for some years, I hoped to have extinguished), yet resolving with myself to give all just satisfaction to modest and sober desires, and to redress all public grievances in Church and State, I hoped, by my freedom and their moderation, to prevent all misunderstandings and miscarriages in this; in which, as I feared, affairs would meet with some passion and prejudice in other men, so I resolved they should find least of them in myself, not doubting but by the weight of reason I should counterpoise the over-balancings of any factions.

I was, indeed, sorry to hear with what partiality and popular heat elections were carried in many places; yet hoping that the gravity and discretion of other gentlemen would allay and fix the Commons to a due temperament, (guiding some men's well-meaning zeal by such rules of moderation as are best both to preserve and restore the health of all states and kingdoms,) no man was better pleased with the convening of this Parliament than myself; who knowing best the largeness of my own heart towards my people's good and just contentment, pleased myself most in that good and firm understanding which would hence grow between me and my people.

All jealousies being laid aside, my own and my children's interests gave me many obligations to seek and preserve the love and welfare of my subjects, the only temporal blessing that is left to the ambition of just monarchs, as their greatest honour and safety, next God's protection. I cared not to lessen myself in some things of my wonted prerogative, since I knew I could be no loser, if I might gain but a recompense in my subjects' affections.

I intended not only to oblige my friends, but mine enemies also, exceeding even the desires of those that were factiously discontented, if they did but pretend to any modest and sober sense.

The odium and offences which some men's rigour or remissness in Church and State had contracted upon my government, I resolved to have expiated by such laws and regulations for the future as might not only rectify what was amiss in practice, but supply what was defective in the constitution, no man having a greater zeal to see religion settled, and preserved in truth, unity, and order, than myself, whom it most concerns both in piety and policy; as knowing that no flames of civil dissensions are more dangerous than those which make religious pretensions the grounds of factions.

I resolved to reform what I should by free and full advice in Parliament be convinced of to be amiss, and to grant whatever my reason and conscience told me was fit to be desired. I wish I had kept myself within those bounds, and not suffered my own judgment to have been overborne in some things, more by others' importunities than their arguments. My confidence had less betrayed myself and my kingdoms to those advantages which some men sought for, who wanted nothing but power and occasion to do mischief.

But our sins being ripe, there was no preventing of God's justice from reaping that glory in our calamities which we robbed Him of in our prosperity.

For Thou, O Lord, hast made us see, that resolutions of future reforming do not always satisfy Thy justice, nor prevent Thy vengeance for former miscarriages.

Our sins have overlaid our hopes. Thou hast taught us to depend on Thy mercies to forgive, not on our purpose to amend.

When Thou hast vindicated Thy glory by Thy judgments, and hast shewed us how unsafe it is to offend Thee, upon presumptions afterwards to please Thee; then I trust Thy mercies will restore those blessings to us, which we have so much abused as to force Thee to deprive us of them.

For want of timely repentance of our sins, Thou givest us cause to repent of those remedies we too late apply.

Yet I do not repent of my calling this last Parliament, because, O Lord, I did it with an upright intention to Thy glory and my people's good.

The miseries which have ensued upon me and my kingdoms, are the just effects of Thy displeasure upon us, and may be yet, through thy mercy, preparative of us to future blessings, and better hearts to enjoy them.

O Lord, though Thou hast deprived us of many former comforts, yet grant me and my people the benefit of our afflictions and Thy chastisements, that Thy rod as well as Thy staff may comfort us. Then shall we dare to account them the strokes not of an enemy, but a father, when Thou givest us those humble affections, that measure of patience in repentance, which becomes Thy children. I shall have no cause to repent the miseries this Parliament hath occasioned, when by them Thou hast brought me and my people unfeignedly to repent of the sins we have committed.

Thy grace is infinitely better with our sufferings, than our peace could be with our sins.

O Thou sovereign Goodness and Wisdom, who over-rulest all our counsels, overrule also all our hearts, that the worse things we suffer by Thy justice, the better we may be by Thy mercy.

As our sins have turned our antidotes into poisons, so let Thy grace turn our poisons into antidotes.

As the sins of our peace disposed us to this unhappy war, so let this war prepare us for Thy blessed peace.

That although I have but troublesome kingdoms here, yet I may attain to that kingdom of peace in my heart and in Thy heaven which Christ hath purchased, and Thou wilt give to Thy servant, though a sinner, for my Saviour's sake. Amen.

II.

UPON THE EARL OF STRAFFORD'S DEATH.

I LOOKED upon my Lord of Strafford as a gentleman whose great abilities might make a prince rather afraid than ashamed to employ him in the greatest affairs of State.

For those were prone to create in him great confidence of undertakings, and this was like enough to betray him to great errors and many enemies; whereof he could not but contract good store, while moving in so high a sphere and with so vigorous a lustre, he must needs, as the sun, raise many envious exhalations, which condensed by a popular odium, were capable to cast a cloud upon the brightest merit and integrity.

Though I cannot in my judgment approve all he did, driven, it may be, by the necessities of times and the temper of that people, more than led by his own disposition to any height and rigour of actions; yet I could never be convinced of any such criminousness in him as willingly to expose his life to the stroke of justice, and malice of his enemies.

I never met with a more unhappy conjecture of affairs than in the business of that unfortunate Earl; when between my own unsatisfiedness in conscience, and a necessity, as some told me, of satisfying the importunities of some people, I was persuaded by those that I think wished me well to choose rather what was safe than what seemed just, preferring the outward peace of my kingdoms with men before that inward exactness of conscience before God.

And, indeed, I am so far from excusing or denying that compliance on my part (for plenary consent it was not) to his destruction, whom in my judgment I thought not, by any clear law, guilty of death, that I never bare any touch of conscience with greater regret; which, as a sign of my repentance, I have often with sorrow confessed both to God and men as an act of so sinful frailty, that it discovered more a fear of man than of God, whose name and place on earth no man is worthy to bear, who will avoid inconveniences of state by acts of so high injustice as no public convenience can expiate or compensate.

I see it a bad exchange to wound a man's own conscience, thereby to salve State sores; to calm the storms of popular discontents by stirring up a tempest in a man's own bosom.

Nor hath God's justice failed in the event and sad consequences to shew the world the fallacy of that maxim, Better one man perish, though unjustly, than the people be displeased or destroyed. For,

In all likelihood, I could never have suffered, with

my people, greater calamities, yet with greater comfort, had I vindicated Strafford's innocency, at least by denying to sign that destructive Bill, according to that justice which my conscience suggested to me, then I have done since I gratified some men's unthankful importunities with so cruel a favour. And I have observed, that those who counselled me to sign that Bill, have been so far from receiving the rewards of such ingratiatings with the people, that no men have been harassed and crushed more than they. He only hath been less vexed by them who counselled me not to consent against the vote of my conscience. I hope God hath forgiven me and them the sinful rashness of that business.

To which being in my soul so fully conscious, those judgments God hath pleased to send upon me are so much the more welcome, as a means, I hope, which His mercy hath sanctified so to me as to make me repent of that unjust act, (for so it was to me,) and for the future to teach me that the best rule of policy is to prefer the doing of justice before all enjoyments, and the peace of my conscience before the preservation of my kingdoms.

Nor hath anything more fortified my resolutions against all those violent importunities which since have sought to gain a like consent from me to acts wherein my conscience is unsatisfied, then the sharp touches I have had for what passed me in my Lord of Strafford's business.

Not that I resolved to have employed him in my

affairs, against the advice of my Parliament; but I would not have had any hand in his death, of whose guiltlessness I was better assured than any man living could be.

Nor were the crimes objected against him so clear, as after a long and fair hearing to give convincing satisfaction to the major part of both Houses, especially that of the Lords, of whom scarce a third part were present when the Bill passed that House. And for the House of Commons, many gentlemen, disposed enough to diminish my Lord of Strafford's greatness and power, yet unsatisfied of his guilt in law, durst not condemn him to die; who, for their integrity in their votes, were, by posting their names, exposed to the popular calumny, hatred, and fury, which grew then so exorbitant in their clamours for justice, (that is to have both myself and the two Houses vote and do as they would have us,) that many, it is thought, where rather terrified to concur with the condemning party than satisfied that of right they ought so to do.

And that after-act, vacating the authority of the precedent for future imitation, sufficiently tells the world that some remorse touched even his most implacable enemies as knowing he had very hard measure, and such as they would be very loth should be repeated to themselves.

This tenderness and regret I find in my soul for having had any hand (and that very unwillingly, God knows) in shedding one man's blood unjustly, though under the colour and formalities of justice and pretences

of avoiding public mischiefs; which may, I hope, be
some evidence before God and man to all posterity
that I am far from bearing justly the vast load and guilt
of all that blood which hath been shed in this unhappy
war, which some men will needs charge on me to ease
their own souls, who am, and ever shall be, more afraid
to take away any man's life unjustly than to lose
my own.

*But Thou, O God of infinite mercies, forgive me that
act of sinful compliance, which hath greater aggravations
upon me than any man, since I had not the least temptation of envy or malice against him, and by my place should
at least so far have been a preserver of him, as to have
denied my consent to his destruction.*

*O Lord, I acknowledge my transgression, and my sin is
ever before me.*

*Deliver me from blood-guiltiness, O God, Thou God of
my salvation, and my tongue shall sing of Thy righteousness.*

*Against Thee have I sinned, and done this evil in Thy
sight, for Thou sawest the contradiction between my heart
and my hand.*

*Yet cast me not away from Thy presence, purge me
with the blood of my Redeemer, and I shall be clean; wash
me with that precious effusion, and I shall be whiter than
snow.*

*Teach me to learn righteousness by Thy judgments, and
to see my frailty in Thy justice. While I was persuaded
by shedding one man's blood to prevent after troubles, Thou*

hast for that, among other sins, brought upon me and upon my kingdoms, great, long, and heavy troubles.

Make me to prefer justice, which is Thy will, before all contrary clamours, which are but the discoveries of man's injurious will.

It is too much that they have once overcome me, to please them by displeasing Thee. O never suffer me, for any reason of State, to go against my reason of conscience, which is highly to sin against Thee, the God of reason, and judge of our consciences.

Whatever, O Lord, Thou seest fit to deprive me of, yet restore unto me the joy of Thy salvation, and ever uphold me with Thy free spirit, which subjects my will to none but Thy light of reason, justice and religion, which shines in my soul; for Thou desirest truth in the inward parts, and integrity in the outward expressions.

Lord, hear the voice of Thy Son's and my Saviour's blood, which speaks better things. O make me and my people to hear the voice of joy and gladness, that the bones which Thou hast broken may rejoice in Thy salvation.

III.

Upon His Majesty's going to the House of Commons.

My going to the House of Commons to demand justice upon the five members, was an act which my enemies loaded with all the obloquies and exasperations they could.

It filled indifferent men with great jealousies and fears; yea, and many of my friends resented it as a motion rising rather from passion than reason, and not guided with such discretion as the touchiness of those times required.

But these men knew not the just motives and pregnant grounds with which I thought myself so furnished, that there needed nothing to such evidence as I could have produced against those I charged save only a free and legal trial, which was all I desired.

Nor had I any temptation of displeasure or revenge against those men's persons further than I had discovered those, as I thought, unlawful correspondences they had used, and engagements they had made, to embroil my kingdoms; all of which I missed but little to have produced writings under some men's own hands who were the chief contrivers of the following innovations.

Providence would not have it so; yet I wanted not such probabilities as were sufficient to raise jealousies in any king's heart, who is not wholly stupid and neglective of the public peace; which to preserve by calling in question half a dozen men in a fair and legal way (which, God knows, was all my design), could have amounted to no worse effect, had it succeeded, than either to do me or my kingdom right, in case they had been found guilty, or else to have cleared their innocency and removed my suspicions, which, as they were not raised out of my malice, so neither were they in reason to be smothered.

What flames of discontent this spark (though I sought by all speedy and possible means to quench it) soon kindled, all the world is witness. The aspersion which some men cast upon that action, as if I had designed by force to assault the House of Commons and invade their privilege, is so false, that as God best knows I had no such intent, so none that attended me could justly gather from anything I then said or did the least intimation of any such thoughts.

That I went attended with some gentlemen, as it was no unwonted thing for the majesty and safety of a king so to be attended, especially in discontented times, so were my followers at that time short of my ordinary guard, and no way proportionable to hazard a tumultary conflict. Nor were they more scared at my coming than I was unassured of not having some affronts cast upon me, if I had none with me to preserve a reverence to me; for many had, at that time, learned to think those hard thoughts which they have since abundantly vented against me both by words and deeds.

The sum of that business was this: those men and their adherents were then looked upon by the affrighted vulgar as greater protectors of their laws and liberties than myself, and so worthier of their protection. I leave them to God and their own consciences, who, if guilty of evil machinations, no present impunity or popular vindications of them will be subterfuge sufficient to rescue them from those exact tribunals.

To which, in the obstructions of justice among men, we must religiously appeal, as being an argument to us

Christians of that after unavoidable judgment which shall rejudge what among men is but corruptly decided, or not at all.

I endeavoured to have prevented, if God had seen fit, those future commotions which I foresaw would in all likelihood follow some men's activity, if not restrained, and so now have done to the undoing of many thousands; the more is the pity.

But to overawe the freedom of the Houses, or to weaken their just authority by any violent impressions upon them, was not at all my design. I thought I had so much justice and reason on my side as should not have needed so rough assistance, and I was resolved rather to bear the repulse with patience than to use such hazarduous extremities.

But Thou, O Lord, art my witness in heaven, and in my heart. If I have purposed any violence or oppression against the innocent, or if there were any such wickedness in my thoughts, then let the enemy persecute my soul, and tread my life to the ground, and lay mine honour in the dust.

Thou that seest not as man seeth, but lookest beyond all popular appearances, searching the heart and trying the reins, and bringing to light the hidden things of darkness, shew Thyself.

Let not my afflictions be esteemed, as with wise and godly men they cannot be, any argument of my sin in that matter, more than their impunity among good men is any sure token of their innocency.

But forgive them wherein they have done amiss, though they are not punished for it in this world.

Save Thy servant from the privy conspiracies and open violence of bloody and unreasonable men, according to the uprightness of my heart and the innocency of my hands in this matter.

Plead my cause, and maintain my right, O Thou that sittest in the throne judging rightly, that Thy servant may rejoice in Thy salvation.

IV.

Upon the Insolency of the Tumults.

I never thought anything, except our sins, more ominously presaging all these mischiefs which have followed, than those tumults in London and Westminster soon after the convening of this Parliament which were not like a storm at sea, (which yet wants not its terror,) but like an earthquake, shaking the very foundation of all; than which nothing in the world hath more of horror.

As it is one of the most convincing arguments that there is a God, while His power sets bounds to the raging of the sea, so it is no less that He restrains the madness of the people. Nor does anything portend more God's displeasure against a nation than when He suffers the confluence and clamours of the vulgar to pass all boundaries of laws and reverence to authority.

Which those tumults did to so high degrees of

insolence, that they spared not to invade the honour
and freedom of the two Houses, menacing, reproaching,
shaking, yea, and assaulting some members of both
Houses as they fancied or disliked them; nor did they
forbear most rude and unseemly deportments, both in
contemptuous words and actions, to myself and my
court.

Nor was this a short fit or two of shaking, as an
ague, but a quotidian fever, always increasing to higher
inflammations, impatient of any mitigation, restraint, or
remission.

First, they must be a guard against those fears which
some men scared themselves and others withal; when,
indeed, nothing was more to be feared, and less to be
used by wise men, than those tumultuary confluxes of
mean and rude people who are taught first to petition,
then to protect, then to dictate, at last to command and
overawe the Parliament.

All obstructions of Parliament, that is, all freedom of
differing in votes, and debating matters with reason
and candour, must be taken away with these tumults.
By these must the Houses be purged, and all rotten
members (as they pleased to count them) cast out; by
these the obstinacy of men, resolved to discharge their
consciences, must be subdued; by these all factious,
seditious, and schismatical proposals against government, ecclesiastical or civil, must be backed and
abetted till they prevailed.

Generally, whoever had most mind to bring forth
confusion and ruin upon Church and State used the

midwifery of those tumults, whose riot and impatience was such as they would not stay the ripening and season of counsels, or fair production of acts, in the order, gravity, and deliberateness befitting a Parliament, but ripped up with barbarous cruelty, and forcibly cut out abortive notes, such as their inviters and encouragers most fancied.

Yea, so enormous and detestable were their outrages, that no sober man could be without infinite shame and sorrow to see them so tolerated and connived at by some, countenanced, encouraged, and applauded by others.

What good man had not rather want anything he most desired for the public good, than obtain it by such unlawful and irreligious means? But men's passions and God's directions seldom agree; violent designs and motions must have suitable engines; such as too much attend their own ends, seldom confine themselves to God's means. Force must crowd in what reason will not lead.

Who were the chief demagogues and patrons of tumults, to send for them, to flatter and embolden them, to direct and tune their clamorous importunities, some men yet living are too conscious to pretend ignorance. God in His due time will let these see that those were no fit means to be used for attaining His ends.

But as it is no strange thing for the sea to rage when strong winds blow upon it, so neither for multitudes to become insolent when they have men of some reputation for parts and piety to set them on.

That which made their rudeness most formidable was, that many complaints being made, and messages sent by myself and some of both Houses yet no order for redress could be obtained with any vigour and efficacy proportionable to the malignity of that now far-spread disease and pre-dominant mischief.

Such was some men's stupidity, that they feared no inconvenience; others' petulancy, that they joyed to see their betters shamefully outraged and abused, while they knew their only security consisted in vulgar flattery, so insensible were they of mine or the two Houses common safety and honours.

Nor could ever any order be obtained impartially to examine, censure, and punish the known *Boutefeus* and impudent incendiaries, who boasted of the influence they had, and used to convoke those tumults as their advantages served.

Yea some, who should have been wiser statesmen, owned them as friends, commending their courage, zeal, and industry, which to sober men could seem no better than that of the devil, who *goes about seeking whom he may* deceive and *devour*.

I confess, when I found such a deafness, that no declaration from the bishops, who were first foully insolenced and assaulted, nor yet from other lords and gentlemen of honour, nor yet from myself, could take place for the due repression of these tumults, and securing not only our freedom in Parliament, but our very persons in the streets; I thought myself not bound by my presence to provoke them to higher boldness and contempts; I hoped by my withdrawing to give time both for the ebbing of their tumultuous fury, and others regaining some degrees of modesty and sober sense.

Some may interpret it as an effect of pusillanimity in any man, for popular terrors, to desert his public station; but I think it is hardiness beyond true valour for a wise man to set himself against the breaking in of a sea, which to resist at present threatens imminent danger, but to withdraw gives it space to spend its fury, and gains a fitter time to repair the breach. Certainly a gallant man had rather fight to great disadvantages for number and place in the field in an orderly way, than scuffle with an undisciplined rabble.

Some suspected and affirmed that I meditated a war, when I went from Whitehall only to redeem my person and conscience from violence: God knows I did not then think of a war. Nor will any prudent man conceive that I would, by so many former and some after acts, have so much weakened myself if I had purposed to engage in a war, which to decline by all means I denied myself in so many particulars. It is evident I had then no army to fly unto for protection and vindication.

Who can blame me, or any other, for withdrawing ourselves from the dailie baitings of the tumults, not knowing whether their fury and discontent might not fly so high as to worry and tear those in pieces whom as yet they but played with in their paws? God, who is my sole judge, is my witness in heaven that I never had any thoughts of my going from my house at Whitehall if I could have had but any reasonable fair quarter. I was resolved to bear much, and did so; but I did not think myself bound to prostitute the majesty of my place and person, the safety of my wife and children, to those who are prone to insult most when they have objects and opportunity most capable of their rudeness and petulancy.

But this business of the tumults, whereof some have given already an account to God, others yet living know themselves desperately guilty, time and the guilt of many has so smothered up and buried, that I think it best to leave it as it is; only I believe the just Avenger of all disorders will in time make those men and that city see their sin in the glass of their punishment. It is more than an even lay, that they may one day see themselves punished by that way they offended.

Had this Parliament, as it was in its first election and constitution, sate full and free, the members of both Houses, being left to their freedom of voting, as in all reason, honour, and religion they should have been, I doubt not but things would have been so carried as would have given no less good content to all good men than they wished or expected.

For I was resolved to hear reason in all things, and to consent to it as far as I could comprehend it; but as swine are to gardens and orderly plantations, so are tumults to Parliaments, and plebian concourses to public counsels, turning all into disorders and sordid confusions.

I am prone sometimes to think that had I called this Parliament to any other place in England, as I might opportunely enough have done, the sad consequences in all likelihood, with God's blessing, might have been prevented. A Parliament would have been welcome in any place; no place afforded such confluence of various and vicious humours as that where it was unhappily convened. But we must leave all to God, who orders our disorders, and magnifies His wisdom most when our follies and miseries are most discovered.

But Thou, O Lord, art my refuge and defence; to Thee I may safely fly, who rulest the raging of the sea, and the madness of the people.

The floods, O Lord, the floods are come in upon me, and are ready to overwhelm me.

I look upon my sins, and the sins of my people, (which are the tumults of our souls against Thee, O Lord) as the just cause of these popular inundations which Thou permittest to overbear all the banks of loyalty, modesty, laws, justice, and religion.

But Thou that gatheredst the waters into one place, and madest the dry land to appear, and after didst assuage the flood which drowned the world by the word of Thy power, rebuke those beasts of the people, and deliver me from the rudeness and strivings of the multitude.

Restore, we beseech Thee, unto us the freedoms of our councils and Parliaments; make us unpassionately to see the light of reason and religion, and with all order and gravity to follow it, as it becomes men and Christians;

so shall we praise Thy Name, who art the God of order and counsel.

What man cannot or will not repress, Thy omnipotent justice can and will.

O Lord, give them that are yet living a timely sense and sorrow for their great sin, whom Thou knowest guilty of raising or not suppressing those disorders. Let shame here, and not suffering hereafter, be their punishment.

Set bounds to our passions by reason, to our errors by truth, to our seditions by laws duly executed, and to our schisms by charity, that we may be, as Thy Jerusalem, a city at unity in itself.

This grant, O my God, in Thy good time, for Jesus Christ's sake. Amen.

V.

Upon His Majesty's Passing the Bill for the Triennial Parliaments, and, after settling this, during the Pleasure of the Two Houses.

THAT the world might be fully confirmed in my purposes at first to contribute what in justice, reason, honour, and conscience I could to the happy success of this Parliament, which had in me no other design but the general good of my kingdoms, I willingly passed the Bill for Triennial Parliaments; which, as gentle and seasonable physic might, if well applied, prevent any distempers from getting any head or prevailing, especially if the remedy proved not a disease beyond all remedy.

I conceived this Parliament would find work, with convenient recesses, for the first three years, but I did not imagine that some men would thereby have occasioned more work than they found to do by undoing so much as they found well done to their hands. Such is some men's activity, that they will needs make work rather than want it, and choose to be doing amiss rather than do nothing.

When that first Act seemed too scanty to satisfy some men's fears, and compass public affairs, I was persuaded to grant that Bill of sitting during the pleasure of the Houses, which amounted in some men's sense to as much as the perpetuating this Parliament. By this act of highest confidence I hoped for ever to shut out and lock the door upon all present jealousies and future mistakes; I confess I did not thereby intend to shut myself out of doors, as some men have now requited me.

True, it was an Act unparalleled by any of my predecessors, yet cannot in reason admit of any worse interpretation than this, of an extreme confidence I had that my subjects would not make ill use of an Act, by which I declared so much to trust them, as to deny myself in so high a point of my prerogative.

For good subjects will never think it just or fit that my condition should be worse by my bettering theirs; nor, indeed, would it have been so in the events if some men had known as well with moderation to use, as with earnestness to desire, advantages of doing good or evil.

A continual Parliament, I thought, would but keep

the common weal in tune, by preserving laws in their due execution and vigour, wherein my interest lies more than any man's, since by those laws my rights as a king would be preserved no less than my subjects, which is all I desired. More than the law gives me I would not have, and less the meanest subject should not.

Some, as I have heard, gave it out that I soon repented me of that settling Act, and many would needs persuade me I had cause so to do; but I could not easily nor suddenly suspect such ingratitude in men of honour, that the more I granted them the less I should have and enjoy with them. I still counted myself undiminished by my largest concessions, if by them I might gain and confirm the love of my people.

Of which I do not yet despair but that God will still bless me with increase of it, when men shall have more leisure and less prejudice, that so with unpassionate representations they may reflect upon those, as I think, not more princely than friendly contributions which I granted towards the perpetuating of their happiness, who are now only miserable in this, that some men's ambition will not give them leave to enjoy what I intended for their good.

Nor do I doubt but that in God's due time the loyal and cleared affections of my people will strive to return such retributions of love and honour to me or my posterity, as may fully compensate both the acts of my confidence and my sufferings for them, which, God knows, have been neither few, nor small, nor short; occasioned chiefly by a persuasion I had that I could not grant too much, or distrust too little, to men that, being professedly my subjects, pretended singular piety and religious strictness.

The injury of all injuries is that which some men will needs load me withal, as if I were a wilful and resolved occasioner of my own and my subjects' miseries; while, as they confidently, but, God knows, falsely divulge, I repining at the establishment of this Parliament, endeavoured by force and open hostility to undo what by my royal assent I had done. Sure it had argued a very short sight of things, and an extreme fatuity of mind in me, so far to bind my own hands at their request, if I had shortly meant to have used a sword against them. God knows, though I had then a sense of injuries, yet not such as to think them worth vindicating by a war. I was not then compelled, as since, to injure myself by their not using favours with the same candour wherewith they were conferred. The tumults, indeed, threatened to abuse all acts of grace and turn them into wantonness; but I thought at length their own fears, whose black arts first raised up those turbulent spirits, would force them to conjure them down again.

Nor, if I had justly resented any indignities put upon me or others, was I then in any capacity to have taken just revenge in an hostile and warlike way upon those whom I knew so well fortified in the love of the meaner sort of the people, that I could not have given my enemies greater and more desired advantages against me than by so unprincely inconstancy to have assaulted them with arms, thereby to scatter them, whom but lately I had solemnly settled by an Act of Parliament.

God knows I longed for nothing more than that myself and my subjects might quietly enjoy the fruits of my many condescendings.

It had been a course full of sin, as well as of hazard and dishonour, for me to go about the cutting up of that by the sword, which I had so lately planted so much, as I thought, to my subjects' content and mine own too, in all probability; if some men had not feared where no fear was, whose security consisted in scaring others.

I thank God I knew so well the sincerity and uprightness of my own heart in passing that great Bill, which exceeded the very thoughts of former times, that although I may seem a less politician to men, yet I need no secret distinctions or evasions before God. Nor had I any reservations in my own soul when I passed it, nor repentings after, till I saw that my letting some men go up to the pinnacle of the temple was a temptation to them to cast me down headlong; concluding that, without a miracle, monarchy itself, together with me, could not but be dashed in pieces by such a precipitous fall as they intended; whom God in mercy forgive, and make them see at length that as many kingdoms as the devil shewed our Saviour, and the glory of them, if they could be at once enjoyed by them, are not worth the gaining by ways of sinful ingratitude and dishonour, which hazards a soul worth more worlds than this hath kingdoms.

But God hath hitherto preserved me, and made me to see that it is no strange thing for men left to their own passions either to do much evil themselves, or abuse the overmuch goodness of others, whereof an ungrateful surfeit is the most desperate and incurable disease.

I cannot say properly that I repent of that act, since I have no reflections upon it as a sin of my will, though an error of too charitable a judgment; only I am sorry other men's eyes should be evil because mine were good.

To Thee, O my God, do I still appeal, whose all-discerning justice sees through all the disguises of men's pretensions, and deceitful darknesses of their hearts.

Thou gavest me a heart to grant much to my subjects, and now I need a heart fitted to suffer much from some of them.

Thy will be done, though never so much to the crossing of ours, even when we hope to do what might be most conformable to Thine and theirs too, who pretended they aimed at nothing else.

Let Thy grace teach me wisely to enjoy as well the frustratings as the fulfillings of my best hopes and most specious desires.

I see while I thought to allay others' fears, I have raised mine own; and by settling them, have unsettled myself.

Thus have they requited me evil for good, and hatred for my good-will towards them.

O Lord, be Thou my pilot in this dark and dangerous storm, which neither admits my return to the port whence I set out, nor my making any other with that safety and honour which I designed.

It is easy for Thee to keep me safe in the love and confidence of my people, nor is it hard for Thee to preserve me amidst the unjust hatred and jealousies of too many, which Thou hast suffered so far to prevail upon me, as to be able to pervert and abuse my acts of greatest indulgence to them, and assurance of them.

But no favours from me can make others more guilty than myself may be, of misusing those many and great ones which Thou, O Lord, hast conferred on me.

I beseech Thee give me and them such repentance as Thou wilt accept, and such grace as we may not abuse.

Make me so far happy as to make a right use of others' abuses, and by their failings of me, to reflect with a reforming displeasure upon my offences against Thee.

So, although for my sins I am by other men's sins deprived of Thy temporal blessings, yet I may be happy to enjoy the comfort of Thy mercies, which often raise the greatest sufferers to be the most glorious saints.

VI.

Upon His Majesty's Retirement from Westminster.

WITH what unwillingness I withdrew from Westminster, let them judge who, unprovided of tackling and victual, are forced to sea by a storm, yet better do so than venture splitting or sinking on a lee-shore.

I stayed at Whitehall till I was driven away by shame more than fear, to see the barbarous rudeness of those tumults who resolved they would take the boldness to demand anything, and not leave either myself or the members of Parliament the liberty of our reason and conscience to deny them anything.

Nor was this intolerable oppression my case alone, though chiefly mine; for the Lords and Commons might be content to be over-voted by the major part of their Houses, when they had used each their own freedom.

Whose agreeing votes were not by any law or reason conclusive to my judgment, nor can they include or carry with them my consent, whom they represent not in any kind; nor am I further bound to agree with the votes of both Houses than I see them agree with the will of God, with my just rights as a King, and the general good of my people. I see that, as many men, they are seldom of one mind; and I may oft see that the major part of them are not in the right.

I had formerly declared to sober and moderate minds how desirous I was to give all just content when I agreed to so many Bills; which had been enough to secure and satisfy all, if some men's hydropic insatiableness had not learned to thirst the more by how much the more they drank, whom no fountain of royal bounty was able to overcome, so resolved they seemed either utterly to exhaust it, or barbarously to obstruct it.

Sure it ceases to be counsel when not reason is used, as to men, to persuade, but force and terror, as to beasts, to drive and compel men to assent to whatever tumultuary patrons shall project. He deserves to be a slave, without pity or redemption, that is content to have the rational sovereignty of his soul and liberty of his will and words so captivated.

Nor do I think my kingdoms so considerable as to preserve them with the forfeiture of that freedom which cannot be denied me as a King, because it belongs to me as a man and a Christian, owning the dictates of none but God above me, as obliging me to consent. Better for me to die enjoying this empire of my soul, which subjects me only to God, so far as by reason or religion He directs me, than live with the title of a king, if it should carry such a vassalage with it as not to suffer me to use my reason and conscience in which I declare as a king to like or dislike.

So far am I from thinking the majesty of the crown of England to be bound by any Coronation Oath, in a blind and brutish formality to consent to whatever its subjects in Parliament shall require, as some men will needs infer, while denying me any power of a negative voice as king, they are not ashamed to seek to deprive me of the liberty of using my reason with a good conscience, which themselves and all the commons of England enjoy proportionable to their influence on the public; who would take it very ill to be urged not to deny whatever myself, as King, or the House of Peers with me, should not so much desire as enjoin them to pass. I think my oath fully discharged in that point by my governing only by such laws as my people, with the House of Peers, have chosen, and myself consented to. I shall never think myself conscientiously tied to go as oft against my conscience as I should consent to such new proposals which my reason, in justice, honour, and religion, bids me deny.

Yet so tender I see some men are of their being subject to arbitrary government, that is, the law of another's will, to which themselves give no consent, that they care not with how much dishonour and absurdity they make their King the only man that must be subject to the will of others, without having power left him to use his own reason, either in person or by any representation.

And if my dissentings at any time were, as some have suspected and uncharitably avowed, out of error, opinionativeness, weakness, or wilfulness, and what they call obstinacy in me, (which not true judgment of things, but some vehement prejudice or passion hath fixed on my mind,) yet can no man think it other than the badge and method of slavery by savage rudeness and importunate obtrusions of violence to have the mist of his error and passion dispelled, which is a shadow of reason, and must serve those that are destitute of the substance. Sure that man cannot be blamable to God or man who seriously endeavours to see the best reason of things, and faithfully follows what he takes for reason. The uprightness of his intentions will excuse the possible failings of his understanding. If a pilot at sea cannot see the pole star, it can be no fault in him to steer his course by such stars as do best appear to him. It argues rather those men to be conscious of their defects of reason and convincing arguments, who call in the assistance of mere force to carry on the weakness of their counsels and proposals. I may in the truth and uprightness of my heart protest before God and men that I never wilfully opposed or denied anything that was in a fair way, after full and free debates, propounded to me by the two Houses, further than I thought in good reason I might and was bound to do.

Nor did anything ever please me more than when my judgment so concurred with theirs, that I might with good conscience consent to them; yea, in many things, where not absolute and moral necessity of reason, but temporary convenience on point of honour was to be considered, I chose rather to deny myself than them, as preferring that which they thought necessary for my people's good before what I saw but convenient for myself.

For I can be content to recede much from my own interests and personal rights, of which I conceive myself to be master, but in what concerns truth, justice, the rights of the Church, my crown, together with the general good of my kingdoms, all which I am bound to preserve as much as morally lies in me, here I am and ever shall be fixed and resolute; nor shall any man gain my consent to that wherein my heart gives my tongue or hand the lie; nor will I be brought to affirm that to men which in my conscience I denied before God. I would rather choose to wear a crown of thorns with my Saviour, than to exchange that of gold, which is due to me, for one of lead, whose embased flexibleness shall be forced to bend and comply to the various and oft contrary dictates of any factions, when instead of reason and public concernments they obtrude nothing but what makes for the interest of parties, and flows from the partialities of private wills and passions.

I know no resolutions more worthy a Christian king, than to prefer his conscience before his kingdoms.

O my God, preserve Thy servant in this native, rational, and religious freedom, for this, I believe, is Thy will that we should maintain; who, though Thou dost justly require us to submit our understandings and wills to Thine, whose wisdom and goodness can neither err nor misguide us, and so far to deny our carnal reason in order to Thy sacred mysteries and commands, that we should believe and obey rather than dispute them; yet dost Thou expect from us only such a reasonable service of Thee, as not to do anything for Thee against our consciences; and as to the desires of men, enjoinest us to try all things by the touchstone of reason and laws, which are the rules of civil justice, and to declare our consent to that only which our judgments approve.

Thou knowest, O Lord, how unwilling I was to desert that place in which thou hast set me, and whereto the affairs of my kingdoms at present do call me.

My people can witness how far I have been content for

their good to deny myself in what Thou hast subjected to my disposal.

O let not the unthankful importunities and tumultuary violence of some men's immoderate demands ever betray me to that degenerous and unmanly slavery, which should make me strengthen them by my consent in those things which I think in my conscience to be against Thy glory, the good of my subjects, and the discharge of my own duty to reason and justice.

Make me willing to suffer the greatest indignities and injuries they press upon me, rather than commit the least sin against my conscience.

Let the just liberties of my people be, as well they may, preserved in fair and equal ways, without the slavery of my soul.

Thou that hast invested me by Thy favours in the power of a Christian king, suffer me not to subject my reason to other men's passions and designs, which to me seem unreasonable, unjust, and irreligious; so shall I serve Thee in the truth and uprightness of my heart, though I cannot satisfy these men.

Though I be driven from among them, yet give me grace to walk always uprightly before Thee.

Lead me in the way of truth and justice, for these, I know, will bring me at last to peace and happiness with Thee, though for these I have much trouble among men.

This I beg of Thee for my Saviour's sake.

VII.

Upon the Queen's Departure and Absence out of England.

ALTHOUGH I have much cause to be troubled at my wife's departure from me and out of my dominions, yet not her absence so much as the scandal of that necessity which drives her away doth afflict me, that she should be compelled by my own subjects, and those pretending to be Protestants, to withdraw for her safety, this being the first example of any Protestant subjects that have taken up arms against their king, a Protestant. For I look upon this now done in England as another act of the same tragedy which was lately begun in Scotland; the brands of that fire, being ill quenched, have kindled the like flames here. I fear such notions, so little to the adornment of the Protestant profession, may occasion a further alienation of mind and divorce of affections in her from that religion, which is the only thing wherein we differ.

Which yet God can, and I pray He would, in time take away, and not suffer these practices to be any obstruction to her judgment, since it is the motion of those men, for the most part, who are yet to seek and settle their religion for doctrine, government, and good manners, and so not to be imputed to the true English Protestants, who continue firm to their former settled principles and laws.

I am sorry my relation to so deserving a lady should be any occasion of her danger and affliction, whose merits would have served her for a protection among the savage Indians, while their rudeness and barbarity knows not so perfectly to hate all virtues as some men's subtilty doth, among whom I yet think few are so malicious as to hate her for herself. The fault is, that she is my wife.

All justice, then, as well as affection commands me to study her security, who is only in danger for my sake. I am content to be tossed, weather-beaten, and shipwrecked, so as she may be in safe harbour.

This comfort I shall enjoy by her safety in the midst of my personal dangers, that I can perish but half if she be preserved; in whose memory and hopeful posterity I may yet survive the malice of my enemies, although they should be satiated with my blood.

I must leave her and them to the love and loyalty of my good subjects, and to His protection who is able to punish the faults of princes, and no less severely to revenge the injuries done to them by those who in all duty and allegiance ought to have made good that safety which the laws chiefly provide for princes.

But common civility is in vain expected from those that dispute their loyalty; nor can it be safe for any relation to a king to tarry among them who are shaking hands with their allegiance, under pretence of laying faster hold on their religion.

It is pity so noble and peaceful a soul should see, much more suffer, the rudeness of those who must make up their want of justice with inhumanity and impudence.

Her sympathy with me in my afflictions will make her virtues shine with greater lustre, as stars in the darkest nights, and assure the envious world that she loves me, not my fortunes.

Neither of us but can easily forgive, since we do not so much blame the unkindness of the generality and vulgar; for we see God is pleased to try both our patience by the most self-punishing sin, the ingratitude of those who, having eaten of our bread and being enriched with our bounty, have scornfully lift up themselves against us: and those of our own household are become our enemies. I pray God lay not their sin to their charge, who think to satisfy all obligations to duty by their corban of religion, and can less endure to see, than to sin against, their benefactors as well as their sovereigns.

But even that policy of my enemies is so far venial, as it was necessary to their designs, by scandalous articles and all irreverent demeanour to seek to drive her out of my kingdoms; lest by the influence of her example—eminent for love as a wife and loyalty as a subject—she should have converted to, or retained in their love and loyalty, all those whom they had a purpose to pervert.

The less I may be blest with her company, the more I will retire to God and my own heart, whence no malice can banish her. My enemies may envy, but they can never deprive me of the enjoyment of her virtues while I enjoy myself.

Thou, O Lord, whose justice at present sees fit to scatter us, let Thy mercy, in Thy due time, re-unite us on earth, if it be Thy will; however, bring us both at last to Thy heavenly kingdom.

Preserve us from the hands of our despiteful and deadly enemies, and prepare us by our sufferings for Thy presence.

Though we differ in some things as to religion, which is my greatest temporal infelicity, yet, Lord, give and accept the sincerity of our affections, which desire to seek, to find, to embrace every truth of Thine.

Let both our hearts agree in the love of Thyself, and Christ crucified for us.

Teach us both what Thou wouldest have us to know in order to Thy glory, our public relations, and our souls' eternal good, and make us careful to do what good we know.

Let neither ignorance of what is necessary to be known, nor unbelief or disobedience to what we know, be our misery or our wilful default.

Let not this great scandal of those my subjects which profess the same religion with me, be any hindrance to her love of any truth Thou wouldst have her to learn, nor any hardening of her in any error Thou wouldst have cleared to her.

Let mine and other men's constancy be an antidote against the poison of their example.

Let the truth of that religion I profess be represented to her judgment with all the beauties of humility, loyalty, charity and peaceableness, which are the proper fruits and ornaments of it; not in the odious disguises of levity, *schism, heresy, novelty, cruelty, and disloyalty, which some men's practices have lately put upon it.*

Let her see Thy sacred and saving truths as Thine, that she may believe, love, and obey them as Thine, cleared from all rust and dross of human mixtures.

That in the glass of Thy truth she may see Thee in those mercies which Thou has offered to us in Thy Son Jesus Christ our only Saviour, and serve Thee in all those holy duties which most agree with His holy doctrine and most imitable example.

The experience we have of the vanity and uncertainty of all human glory and greatness in our scatterings and eclipses, let it make us both so much the more ambitious to be invested in those durable honours and perfections which are only to be found in Thyself, and obtained through Jesus Christ.

VIII.

Upon His Majesty's Repulse at Hull, and the Fates of the Hothams.

My repulse at Hull seemed at the first view an act of so rude disloyalty, that my greatest enemies had scarce confidence enough to abet or own it. It was the first overt essay to be made how patiently I could bear the loss of my kingdoms.

God knows it affected me more with shame and sorrow for others than with anger for myself; nor did the affront done to me trouble me so much as their sin, which admitted no colour or excuse.

I was resolved how to bear this and much more with patience; but I foresaw they could hardly contain themselves within the compass of this one unworthy act, who had effrontery enough to commit or countenance it. This was but the hand of that cloud which was soon after to overspread the whole kingdom, and cast all into disorder and darkness.

For it is among the wicked maxims of bold and disloyal undertakers, that bad actions must always be seconded with worse, and rather not be begun, than not carried on, for they think the retreat more dangerous than the assault, and hate repentance more than perseverance in a fault.

This gave me to see clearly through all the pious disguises and soft palliations of some men, whose words were sometimes smoother than oil, but now I saw they would prove very swords.

Against which I having, as yet, no defence, but that of a good conscience, thought it my best policy with patience to bear what I could not remedy. And in this I thank God, I had the better of Hotham, that no disdain or emotion of passion transported me by the indignity of his carriage, to do or say anything unbeseeming myself, or unsuitable to that temper which in greatest injuries I think best becomes a Christian, as coming nearest to the great example of Christ.

And indeed I desire always more to remember I am a Christian than a king, for what the majesty of the one might justly abhor, the charity of the other is willing to bear; what the height of a king tempteth to revenge, the humility of a Christian teacheth to forgive. Keeping in compass all those impotent passions, whose excess injures a man more than his greatest enemies can, for these give their malice a full impression on our souls, which otherways cannot reach very far, nor do us much hurt.

I cannot but observe how God, not long after, so pleaded and avenged my cause in the eye of the world, that the most wilfully blind cannot avoid the displeasure to see it, and with some remorse and fear to own it as a notable stroke and prediction of divine vengeance.

For Sir John Hotham, unreproached, unthreatened, uncursed by any secret language or imprecation of mine, only blasted with the conscience of his own wickedness, and falling from one inconstancy to another, not long after pays his own and his eldest son's heads as forfeitures of their disloyalty, to those men from whom surely he might have expected another reward than thus to divide their heads from their bodies, whose hearts with them were divided from their king.

Nor is it strange that they who employed them at first in so high a service, and so successful to them, should not find mercy enough to forgive him who had so much premerited of them, for apostacy unto loyalty some men account the most unpardonable sin.

Nor did a solitary vengeance serve the turn; the cutting off one head in a family is not enough to expiate the affront done to the head of the Commonweal. The eldest son must be involved in the punishment, as he was infected with the sin of the father against the father of his country; root and branch God cuts off in one day.

These observations are obvious to every fancy. God knows I was so far from rejoicing in the Hothams' ruin (though it were such as was able to give the greatest thirst for revenge a full draught, being executed by them who first employed him against me,) that I so far pitied him, as I thought he at first acted more against the light of his conscience than I hope many other men do in the same cause.

For he was never thought to be of that superstitious sourness which some men pretend to in matters of religion, which so darkens their judgment that they cannot see anything of sin and rebellion in those means they use, with intents to reform to their models of what they call religion, who think all is gold of piety which doth but glitter with a show of zeal and fervency.

Sir John Hotham was, I think, a man of another temper, and so most liable to those downright temptations of ambition which have no cloak or cheat of religion to impose upon themselves or others.

That which makes me more pity him is, that after he began to have some inclinations towards a repentance for his sin, and reparation of his duty to me, he should be so unhappy as to fall into the hands of their justice, and not my mercy, who would as willingly have forgiven him as he could have asked that favour of me.

For I think clemency a debt which we ought to pay to those that crave it, when we have cause to believe that they would not after abuse it, since God Himself suffers us not to pay anything for His mercy, but only prayers and praises.

Poor gentleman, he is now become a noteable monument of unprosperous disloyalty, teaching the world by so sad and unfortunate a spectacle, that the rude carriage of a subject towards his sovereign carries always its own vengeance as an unseparable shadow with it: and those oft prove the most fatal and implacable executioners of it, who were the first employers in the service.

Aftertimes will dispute it whether Hotham were more infamous at Hull or at Tower-hill, though it is certain that no punishment so stains a man's honour as wilful perpetrations of unworthy actions; which besides the conscience of the sin, brand with the most indelible characters of infamy the name and memory to posterity, who, not engaged in the factions of the times, have the most impartial reflection on the actions.

But Thou, O Lord, who hast in so remarkable a way avenged Thy servant, suffer me not to take any secret pleasure in it; for as his death hath satisfied the injury he did to me, so let me not by it gratify any passion in me, lest I make Thy vengeance to be mine, and consider the affront against me more than the sin against Thee.

Thou, indeed, without any desire or endeavour of mine, hast made his mischief to return on his own head, and his violent dealing to come down on his own pate.

Thou hast pleaded my cause, even before the sons of men, and taken the matter into Thine own hands, that men may know it was Thy work, and see that Thou, Lord, hast done it.

I do not, I dare not say, so let mine enemies perish, O Lord; yea, Lord, rather give them repentance, pardon, and impunity if it be Thy blessed will.

Let not Thy justice prevent the objects and opportunities of my mercy; yea, let them live and amend who have most offended me in so high a nature, that I may have those to forgive who bear most proportion in their offences to those trespasses against Thy majesty, which I hope Thy mercy hath forgiven me.

Lord, lay not their sins (who yet live) to their charge for condemnation, but to their consciences for amendment. Let the lightning of this thunderbolt, which hath been so severe a punishment to one, be a terror to all.

Discover to them their sin, who know not they have done amiss, and scare them from their sin, that sin of malicious wickedness.

That preventing Thy judgments by their true repentance they may escape the strokes of Thine eternal vengeance.

And do Thou, O Lord, establish the throne of Thy servant in mercy and truth meeting together. Let my crown ever flourish in righteousness and peace kissing each other.

Hear my prayer, O Lord, who has taught us to pray for, to do good to, and to love our enemies for Thy sake, who hast prevented us with overtures of Thy love, even when we were Thine enemies, and hast sent Thy Son Jesus Christ to die for us when we were disposed to crucify Him.

IX.

Upon the Lifting and Raising Armies against the King.

I FIND that I am at the same point and posture I was when they forced me to leave Whitehall. What tumults could not do, an army must, which is but tumults lifted and enrolled to a better order, but as bad an end. My recess hath given them confidence that I may be conquered.

And so I easily may as to any outward strength, which, God knows, is little, or none at all; but I have a soul invincible, through God's grace enabling me. Here I am sure to be a conqueror, if God will give me such a measure of constancy as to fear Him more than man, and to love the inward peace of my conscience before any outward tranquility.

And must I be opposed with force, because they have not reason wherewith to convince me? O my soul, be of good courage. They confess their known weakness as to truth and justice who choose rather to contend by armies than by arguments.

Is this the reward and thanks that I am to receive for those many acts of grace I have lately passed, and for those many indignities I have endured? Is there no way left to make me a glorious King, but by my sufferings?

It is a hard and disputable choice for a King that loves his people, and desires their love, either to kill his own subjects, or to be killed by them.

Are the hazards and miseries of civil war in the bowels of my most flourishing kingdom, the fruits I must now reap after seventeen years living and reigning among them with such a measure of justice, peace, plenty, and religion, as all nations about either admired or envied? Notwithstanding some miscarriages in government, which might escape rather through ill counsel of some men driving on their private ends, or the peevishness of others, envying the public should be managed without them, or the hidden and insuperable necessities of State, than any propensity, I hope, of myself either to injuriousness or oppression.

Whose innocent blood during my reign have I shed to satisfy my lust, anger, or covetousness? What widows' or orphans' tears can witness against me, the just cry of which must now be avenged with my own blood? for the hazards of war are equal, nor doth the cannon know any respect of persons.

In vain is my person excepted by a parenthesis of words, when so many hands are armed against me with swords.

God knows how much I have studied to see what ground of justice is alleged for this war against me, that so I might, by giving just satisfaction, either prevent or soon end so unnatural a motion; which, to many men, seems rather the production of a surfeit of peace and wantonness of minds, or of private discontents, ambition, and faction, which easily find or make causes of quarrel, than any real obstructions of public justice, of Parliamentary privilege.

But this is pretended, and this I must be able to avoid and answer before God in my own conscience, however some men are not willing to believe me, lest they should condemn themselves.

When I first withdrew from Whitehall to see if I could allay the insolency of the tumults, of the not suppressing of which no account in reason can be given, where an orderly guard was granted, but only to oppress both mine and the two Houses' freedom of declaring and voting according to every man's conscience, what obstructions of Justice were there further than this, that what seemed just to one man might not seem so to another.

Whom did I by power protect against the justice of Parliament.

That some men withdrew who feared the partiality of their trial, warned by my Lord of Strafford's death, while the vulgar threatened to be their oppressors, and judgers of their judges, was from that instinct which is in all creatures to preserve themselves. If any others refused to appear, where they evidently saw the current of justice and freedom so stopped and troubled by the rabble, that their lawful judges either durst not come to the Houses, or not declare their sense with liberty and safety, it cannot seem strange to any reasonable man, when the sole exposing them to the public odium was enough to ruin them before their cause could be heard or tried.

Had not factious tumults overborne the freedom and honour of the two Houses; had they asserted their justice against them, and made the way open for all the members quietly to come and declare their consciences, I know no man so dear to me whom I had the least inclination to advise either to withdraw himself, or deny appearing upon their summons, to whose sentence according to law I think every subject bound to stand.

Distempers, indeed, were risen to so great a height, for want of timely repressing the vulgar insolences, that the greatest guilt of those which were voted and demanded as delinquents was this, that they would not suffer themselves to be overawed with the tumults and their patrons, nor compelled to abet by their suffrages or presence the designs of those men who agitated innovations and ruin both in Church and State.

In this point I could not but approve their generous constancy and cautiousness; further than this I did never allow any man's refractoriness against the privileges and orders of the Houses, to whom I wished nothing more than safety, fulness, and freedom.

But the truth is, some men, and those not many, despairing in fair and parliamentary ways, by free deliberations and votes, to gain the concurrence of the major part of Lords and Commons, betook themselves by the desperate activity of factious tumults, to sift and terrify away all those members whom they saw to be of contrary minds to their purposes.

How oft was the business of the bishops, enjoying their ancient places and undoubted privileges in the Houses of Peers, carried for them by far the major part of lords. Yet after five repulses, contrary to all order and custom, it was by tumultuary instigations obtruded again, and by a few carried, when most of the peers were forced to absent themselves.

In like manner was the Bill against root and branch brought on by tumultuary clamours and schismatical terrors, which could never pass till both Houses were sufficiently thinned and overawed.

To which partiality, while in all reason, justice, and religion, my conscience forbids me by consenting to make up their votes to Acts of Parliament, I must now be urged with an army, and constrained either to hazard my own and my kingdom's ruin by my defence, or prostrate my conscience to the blind obedience of those men, whose zealous superstition thinks or pretends they cannot do God and the Church a greater service than utterly to destroy that primitive, apostolical, and anciently universal government of the Church by bishops.

Which if other men's judgments bind them to maintain, or forbid them to consent to the abolishing of it, mine much more; who, besides the grounds I have in my judgment, have also a most strict and indispensable oath upon my conscience to preserve that order and the rights of the Church; to which most sacrilegious and abhorred perjury, most unbeseeming a Christian king, should I ever, by giving my consent, be betrayed, I should account it infinitely greater misery than any hath or can befall me, inasmuch as the least sin hath more evil in it than the greatest affliction. Had I gratified the anti-episcopal faction at first in this point with my consent, and sacrificed the ecclesiastical government and revenues to the fury of their covetousness, ambition, and revenge, I believe they would then have found no colourable necessity of raising an army to fetch in and punish delinquents.

That I consented to the Bill of putting the bishops out of the House of Peers, was done with a firm persuasion of their contentedness to suffer a present diminution in their rights and honour for my sake and the commonweal's; which I was confident they would readily yield unto rather than occasion, by the least obstruction on their part, any danger to me or to my kingdom. That I cannot add my consent for the total extirpation of that government (which I have often offered to all fit regulations,) hath so much further tie upon my conscience, as what I think religious and apostolical, and so very sacred and divine, is not to be dispensed with or destroyed, when what is only of civil favour and privilege of honour granted to men of that order, may, with their consent who are concerned in it, be annulled.

This is the true state of those obstructions pretended to be in point of justice and authority of Parliament, when, I call God to witness, I knew none of such consequence as was worth speaking of to make a war, being only such as justice, reason, and religion, had made in my own and other men's consciences.

Afterwards, indeed, a great show of delinquents was made, which were but consequences necessarily following upon mine or others' withdrawing from or defence against violence; but those could not be the first occasion of raising an army against me. Wherein 1 was so far from preventing them (as they have declared often, that they might seem to have the advantage and justice of the defensive part, and load me with all the envy and injuries of first assaulting them), that God knows I had not so much as any hopes of an army in my thoughts. Had the tumults been honourably and effectually repressed by exemplary justice, and the liberty of the Houses so vindicated that all members of either House might with honour and freedom, becoming such a senate, have come and discharged their consciences, I had obtained all that I designed by my withdrawing, and had much more willingly and speedily returned than I retired; this being my necessity driving, the other my choice desiring.

But some men knew I was like to bring the same judgment and constancy which I carried with me, which would never fit their designs; and so while they invited me to come, and grievously complained of my absence, yet they could not but be pleased with it, especially when they had found out that plausible and popular pretext of raising an army to fetch in delinquents, when all that while they never punished the greatest and most intolerable delinquency of the tumults and their exciters, which drave myself and so many of both Houses from their places by most barbarous indignities; which yet in all reason and honour they were as loth to have deserted as those others were willing they should, that so they might have occasion to persecute them with the injuries of an army for not suffering more tamely the injuries of the tumults.

That this is the true state and first drift and design in raising an army against me, is by the sequel so evident, that all other pretences vanish. For when they declared by propositions or treaties what they would have to appease them, there was nothing of consequence offered to me, or demanded of me, as any original difference in any point of law or order of justice. But among other lesser innovations this chiefly was urged, the abolition of Episcopal, and the establishment of Presbyterian government.

All other things at any time propounded were either impertinent as to any ground of a war, or easily granted by me, and only to make up a number, or else they were merely consequential and necessary after the war was by them unjustly begun.

I cannot hinder other men's thoughts, whom the noise and show of piety and heat for reformation and religion might easily so fill with prejudice, that all equality and clearness of judgment might be obstructed. But this was, and is, as to my best observation, the true state of affairs between us when they first raised an army, with this design, either to stop my mouth or to force my consent. And in this truth, as to my conscience, (who was, God knows, as far from meditating a war, as I was in the eye of the world from having any preparation for one,) I find that comfort that in the midst of all the unfortunate successes of this war on my side, I do not think my innocency any whit prejudiced or darkened, nor am I without that integrity and peace before God as with humble confidence to address my prayer to Him.

For Thou, O Lord, seest clearly through all the cloudings of human affairs; Thou judgest without prejudice; Thy omniscience eternally guides Thy unerrable judgment.

O my God, the proud are risen against me, and the assemblies of violent men have sought after my soul, and have not set Thee before their eyes.

Consider my enemies, O Lord, for they are many, and they hate me with a deadly hatred without a cause.

For Thou knowest I had no passion, design, or preparation to embroil my kingdoms in a civil war, whereto I had least temptation, as knowing I must adventure more than any, and could gain least of any by it.

Thou, O Lord, art my witness how oft I have deplored and studied to divert the necessity thereof, wherein I cannot well be thought so prodigally thirsty of my subjects' blood as to venture my own life, which I have been oft compelled to do in this unhappy war, and which were better spent to save than to destroy my people.

O Lord, I need much of Thy grace, with patience, to bear the many afflictions Thou hast suffered some men to bring upon me, but much more to bear the unjust reproaches of those who, not content that I suffer most by the war, will needs persuade the world that I have raised it first, or given just cause to raise it.

The confidence of some men's false tongues is such that they would make me almost suspect my own innocency;

yea, I could be content (at least by my silence) to take upon me so great a guilt before men, if by that I might allay the malice of my enemies, and redeem my people from this miserable war, since Thou, O Lord, knowest my innocency in this thing.

Thou wilt find out bloody and deceitful men, many of whom have not lived out half their days, in which they promised themselves the enjoyment of the fruits of their violent and wicked counsels.

Save, O Lord, Thy servant, as hitherto Thou hast, and in Thy due time scatter the people that delight in war.

Arise, O Lord, lift up Thyself, because of the rage of mine enemies, which increaseth more and more. Behold them that have conceived mischief, travailed with iniquity, and brought forth falsehood.

Thou knowest the chief design of this war is, either to destroy my person, or force my judgment, and to make me revenge my conscience and Thy truth.

I am driven to cross David's choice, and desire rather to fall into the hands of men by denying them (though their mercies be cruel), than into Thy hands, by sinning against my conscience, and in that against Thee, who art a consuming fire. Better they destroy me, than Thou shouldst damn me.

Be Thou ever the defence of my soul, who wilt save the upright in heart.

If nothing but my blood will satisfy my enemies, or quench the flames of my kingdoms or Thy temporal justice, I am content, if it be Thy will, that it be shed by my own subjects' hands.

But O let the blood of me, though their king yet a sinner, be washed with the blood of my innocent and peace-making Redeemer, for in that Thy justice will find not only a temporary expiation, but an eternal plenary satisfaction, both for my sins and the sins of my people, whom I beseech Thee still own for Thine; and when Thy wrath is appeased by my death, O remember Thy great mercies toward them, and forgive them, O my Father, for they know not what they do.

X.

UPON THEIR SEIZING THE KING'S MAGAZINES, FORTS, NAVY, AND MILITIA.

How UNTRULY I am charged with the first raising of an army and beginning this civil war, the eyes that only pity me, and the loyal hearts that durst only pray for me at first, might witness, which yet appear not so many on my side as there were men in arms lifted against me. My unpreparedness for a war may well dishearten those that would help me; while it argues truly my unwillingness to fight, yet it testifies for me that I am set on the defensive part, having so little hopes or power to offend others, that I have none to defend myself, or to preserve what is mine own from their prereption.

No man can doubt but they prevented me in their purposes as well as their injuries, who are so much beforehand in their preparations against me, and surprisals of my strength. Such as are not for them, yet dare not be for me, so overawed is their loyalty by the others' numbers and terrors. I believe my innocency, and unpreparedness to assert my rights and honour, makes me the more guilty in their esteem; who would not so easily have declared a war against me, if I had first assaulted them.

They knew my chiefest arms left me were those only which the ancient Christians were wont to use against their persecutors—prayers and tears. These may serve a good man's turn, if not to conquer as a soldier, yet to suffer as a martyr.

Their preventing of me, and surprising my castles, forts, arms, and navy, with the militia, is so far best for me, that it may drive me from putting any trust in the arm of flesh, and wholly to cast myself into the protection of the living God, who can save by few, or none, as well as by many.

He that made the greedy ravens to be Elias's caterers, and bring him food, may also make their surprisal of outward force and defence an opportunity to shew me the special support of His power and protection.

I thank God I reckon not now the want of the militia so much in reference to my own protection, as my people's.

Their many and sore oppressions grieve me; I am above my own: what I want in the hands of force and power, I have in the wings of faith and prayer.

But this is the strange method these men will needs take, to resolve their riddle of making me a glorious king by taking away my kingly power. Thus I shall become a support to my friends and a terror to my enemies, by being unable to succour the one or suppress the other.

For thus have they designed and proposed to me the new modelling of sovereignty and kingship, as without any reality of power, so without any necessity of subjection and obedience; that the majesty of the kings of England might hereafter hang, like Mahomet's tomb, by a magnetic charm, between the power and privileges of the two Houses, in an airy imagination of regality.

But I believe the surfeit of too much power which some men have greedily seized on, and now seek wholly to devour, will ere long make the commonwealth sick both of it and them, since they cannot well digest it, sovereign power in subjects seldom agreeing with the stomachs of fellow-subjects.

Yet I have, even in this point of the constant militia, sought, by satisfying their fears and importunities, both to secure my friends and overcome mine enemies, to gain the peace of all by depriving myself of a sole power to help or hurt any; yielding the militia (which is my undoubted right no less than the crown) to be disposed of as the two Houses shall think fit during my time.

So willing am I to bury all jealousies in them of me, and to live above all jealousies of them as to myself; I desire not to be safer than I wish them and my people. If I had the sole actual disposing of the militia, I could not protect my people further than they protected me and themselves, so that the use of the militia is mutual. I would but defend myself so far as to be able to defend my good subjects from those men's violence and fraud, who, conscious to their own evil merits and designs, will needs persuade the world that none but wolves are fit to be trusted with the custody of the shepherd and his flock. Miserable experience hath taught my subjects, since power hath been wrested from me and employed against me and them, that neither can be safe, if both be not in such a way as the law hath entrusted the public safety and welfare.

Yet even this concession of mine as to the exercise of the militia, so vast and large, is not satisfactory to some men, which seem to be enemies not to me only, but to all monarchy, and are resolved to transmit to posterity such jealousies of the crown as they should never permit it to enjoy its just and necessary rights in point of power, to which, at last, all law is resolved, while thereby it is best protected.

But here honour and justice due to my successors forbid me to yield to such a total alienation of that power from them, which civility and duty, no less than justice and honour, should have forbad them to have asked of me.

For although I can be content to eclipse my own beams to satisfy their fears, who think they must needs be scorched or blinded if I should shine in the full lustre of kingly power wherewith God and the laws have invested me; yet I will never consent to put out the sun of sovereignty to all posterity and succeeding kings, whose just recovery of their rights from unjust usurpations and extortions shall never be prejudiced or obstructed by any act of mine; which indeed would not be more injurious to succeeding kings than to my subjects, whom I desire to leave in a condition not wholly desperate for the future; so as by a law to be ever subjected to those many factious distractions which must needs follow the many-headed hydra of government; which, as it makes a show to the people to have more eyes to foresee, so they will find it hath more mouths, too, which must be satisfied; and, at best, it hath rather a monstrosity than anything of perfection beyond that of right monarchy, where counsel may be in many, as the senses, but the supreme power can be but in one, as the head.

Haply, when men have tried the horrors and malignant influence which will certainly follow my enforced darkness and eclipse (occasioned by the interposition and shadow of that body which, as the moon, receiveth its chiefest light from me), they will at length more esteem and welcome the restored glory and blessing of the sun's light.

And if at present I may seem, by my receding so much from the use of my right in the power of the militia, to come short of the discharge of that trust to which I am sworn for my people's protection, I conceive those men are guilty of the enforced perjury (if so it may seem), who compel me to take this new and strange way of discharging my trust by seeming to desert it; of protecting my subjects by exposing myself to danger or dishonour for their safety and quiet.

Which in the conflicts of civil war, and advantages of power, cannot be effected but by some side yielding ; to which the greatest love of the public peace, and the firmest assurance of God's protection, arising from a good conscience, doth more invite me, than can be expected from other men's fears, which arising from the injustice of their actions, though never so successful, yet dare not adventure their authors upon any other way of safety than that of the sword and militia ; which yet are but weak defences against the strokes of divine vengeance, which will overtake, or of men's own consciences, which always attend injurious perpetrations.

For myself, I do not think that I can want anything which providential necessity is pleased to take from me, in order to my people's tranquillity and God's glory, whose protection is sufficient for me ; and He is able, by His being with me, abundantly to compensate to me, as He did to Job, whatever honour, power, or liberty the Chaldeans, Sabæans, or the devil himself can deprive me of.

Although they take from me all defence of arms and militia, all refuge by land of forts and castles, all flight by sea in my ships and navy; yea, though they study to rob me of the hearts of my subjects, the greatest treasure and best ammunition of a king, yet cannot they deprive me of my own innocency or God's mercy, nor obstruct my way to heaven.

Therefore, O my God, to Thee I fly for help; if Thou

wilt be on my side, I shall have more with me than can be against me.

There is none in heaven or in earth that I desire in comparison of Thee. In the loss of all, be Thou more than all to me. Make haste to succour, Thou that never failest them that put their trust in Thee.

Thou seest I have no power to oppose them that come against me, who are encouraged to fight under the pretence of fighting for me. But my eyes are toward Thee.

Thou needest no help, nor shall I, if I may have Thine; if not to conquer, yet at least to suffer.

If Thou delightest not in my safety and prosperity, behold here I am, willing to be reduced to what Thou wilt have me, whose judgments oft begin with Thy own children.

I am content to be nothing, that Thou mayest be all.

Thou hast taught me that no king can be saved by the multitude of an host; but yet Thou canst save me by the multitude of Thy mercies, who art the Lord of Hosts, and the Father of mercies.

Help me, O Lord, who am sore distressed on every side; yet be Thou on my side, and I shall not fear what man can do unto me.

I will give Thy justice the glory of my distress.

O let Thy mercy have the glory of my deliverance from them that persecute my soul.

By my sins have I fought against Thee, and robbed Thee of Thy glory, who am Thy subject; and justly mayst Thou by my own subjects strip me of my strength, and eclipse my glory.

But shew Thyself, O my hope and only refuge. Let not mine enemies say, There is no help for him in his God.

Hold up my goings in Thy paths, that my footsteps slip not.

Keep me as the apple of Thine eye, hide me under the shadow of Thy wings.

Shew Thy marvellous loving-kindness, O Thou that savest by Thy right hand them that put their trust in Thee, from those that rise up against them; from the wicked that oppress me, from my deadly enemies that compass me about.

Shew me the path of life; in Thy presence is fulness of joy, at Thy right hand there are pleasures for evermore.

XI.

Upon the Nineteen Propositions first sent to the King, and more afterwards.

ALTHOUGH there be many things they demand, yet if these be all, I am glad to see at what price they set my own safety and my people's peace, which I cannot think I buy at too dear a rate, save only the parting with my conscience and honour. If nothing else will satisfy, I must choose rather to be as miserable and inglorious as my enemies can make or wish me.

Some things here propounded to me have been offered by me, others are easily granted; the rest, I think, ought not to be obtruded upon me with the point of the sword, nor urged with the injuries of a war, when

I have already declared that I cannot yield to them without violating my conscience. It is strange there can be no method of peace but by making war upon my soul.

Here are many things required of me, but I see nothing offered to me by the way of grateful exchange of honour, or any requital for those favours I have or can yet grant them.

This honour they do me, to put me on the giving part, which is more princely and divine. They cannot ask more than I can give, may I but reserve to myself the incommunicable jewel of my conscience, and not be forced to part with that whose loss nothing can repair or requite.

Some things which they are pleased to propound seem unreasonable to me; and while I have any mastery of my reason, how can they think I can consent to them, who know they are such as are inconsistent with being either a king or a good Christian? My yielding so much as I have already makes some men confident I will deny nothing.

The love I have of my people's peace, hath, indeed, great influence upon me; but the love of truth and inward peace hath more.

Should I grant some things they require, I should not so much weaken my outward state of a king as wound that inward quiet of my conscience, which ought to be, is, and ever shall be, by God's grace, dearer to me than my kingdoms.

Some things which a king might approve, yet in

honour and policy are at some times to be denied to some men, lest he should seem not to dare to deny anything, and give too much encouragement to unreasonable demands and importunities.

But to bind myself to a general and implicit consent to whatever they shall desire or propound (for such is one of their propositions), were such a latitude of blind obedience as never was expected from any freeman, nor fit to be required of any man, much less of a king by his own subjects, any of whom he may possibly exceed as much in wisdom as he doth in place and power.

This were as if Samson should have consented, not only to bind his own hands and cut off his hair, but to put out his own eyes, that the Philistines might with the more safety mock and abuse him; which they chose rather to do than quite to destroy him, when he was become so tame an object, and fit occasion for their sport and scorn.

Certainly, to exclude all power of denial seems an arrogancy least of all becoming those who pretend to make their addresses in an humble and loyal way of petitioning; who by that sufficiently confess their own inferiority, which obligeth them to rest, if not satisfied, yet quieted with such an answer as the will and reason of their superior thinks fit to give; who is acknowledged to have a freedom and power of reason to consent or dissent; else it were very foolish and absurd to ask, what another having not liberty to deny, neither hath power to grant.

But if this be my right, belonging to me in reason as

a man, and in honour as a sovereign king (as undoubtedly it doth), how can it be other than extreme injury to confine my reason to a necessity of granting all they have a mind to ask, whose minds may be as differing from mine both in reason and honour, as their aims may be and their qualities are? Which last, God and the laws have sufficiently distinguished, making me their sovereign and them my subjects, whose propositions may soon prove violent oppositions, if once they gain to be necessary impositions upon the regal authority, since no man seeks to limit and confine his King in reason, who hath not a secret aim to share with him, or usurp upon him in power and dominion.

But they would have me trust to their moderation, and abandon mine own discretion; that so I might verify what representations some have made of me to the world, that I am fitter to be their pupil than their prince. Truly I am not so confident of my own sufficiency as not willingly to admit the counsel of others; but yet I am not so diffident of myself as brutishly to submit to any men's dictates, and at once to betray the sovereignty of reason in my soul and the majesty of my own crown to any of my subjects.

Least of all have I any ground of credulity to induce me fully to submit to all the desires of those men who will not admit, or do refuse and neglect to vindicate, the freedom of their own and others' sitting and voting in Parliament.

Besides, all men that know them know this, how young statesmen the most part of these propounders are; so that till experience of one seven years hath shewed me how well they can govern themselves, and so much power as is wrested from me, I should be very foolish indeed, and unfaithful in my trust, to put the reins of both reason and government wholly out of my own into their hands, whose driving is already too much like Jehu's, and whose forwardness to ascend the throne of supremacy portends more of Phaeton than of Phœbus. God divert the omen, if it be His will.

They may remember that at best they sit in Parliament as my subjects, not my superiors; called to be my counsellors, not dictators. Their summons extends to recommend their advice, not to command my duty.

When I first heard of Propositions to be sent me, I expected either some good laws, which had been antiquated by the course of time, or overlaid by the corruption of manners, had been desired to a restoration of their vigour and due execution; or some evil customs preterlegal and abuses personal had been to be removed; or some injuries done by myself and others to the commonweal were to be repaired; or some equable overtures were to be tendered to me, wherein the advantages of my crown being considered by them, might fairly induce me to condescend to what tended to my subjects' good, without any great diminution of myself, whom nature, law, reason, and religion, bind me, in the first place to preserve, without which it is impossible to preserve my people, according to my place.

Or, at least, I looked for such moderate desires of due reformation of what was, indeed, amiss in Church and State, as might still preserve the foundation and essentials of government in both, nor shake and quite overthrow either of them, without any regard to the laws in force, the wisdom and piety of former Parliaments, the ancient and universal practice of Christian Churches, the rights and privileges of particular men; nor yet anything offered in lieu or in the room of what must be destroyed, which might at once reach the good end of the other's institution, and also supply its pretended defects, reform its abuses, and satisfy sober and wise men, not with soft and specious words, pretending zeal and special piety, but with pregnant and solid reasons, both divine and human, which might justify the abruptness and necessity of such vast alterations.

But in all their Propositions I can observe little of these kinds, or to these ends; nothing of any laws disjointed which are to be restored, of any right invaded, of any justice to be unobstructed, of any compensations to be made, of any impartial reformation to be granted; to all or any of which, reason, religion, true policy, or any other human motives might induce me.

But as to the main matters propounded by them at any time, in which is either great novelty or difficulty, I perceive that what were formerly looked upon as factions in the State and schisms in the Church, and so punishable by the laws, have now the confidence, by vulgar clamours and assistance chiefly, to demand not only tolerations of themselves in their vanity, novelty, and confusion, but also abolition of the laws against them, and a total extirpation of that government whose rights they have a mind to invade.

This as to the main. Other Propositions are, for the most part, but as waste paper, in which those are wrapped up to present them somewhat more handsomely.

Nor do I so much wonder at the variety and horrible novelty of some Propositions, there being nothing so monstrous which some fancies are not prone to long for.

This casts me into not an admiration, but an ecstasy, how such things should have the fortune to be propounded in the name of the two Houses of the Parliament of England, among whom I am very confident there was not a fourth part of the members of either House, whose judgments—free, single, and apart—did approve or desire such destructive changes in the government of the Church.

I am persuaded there remains in far the major part of both Houses, if free and full, so much learning, reason, religion, and just moderation, as to know how to sever between the use and the abuse of things, the institution and the corruption, the government and the mis-government, the primitive patterns and the aberrations or blottings of after-copies.

Sure they could not all, upon so little or no reason as yet produced to the contrary, so soon renounce all regard to the laws in force, to antiquity, to the piety of their reforming progenitors, to the prosperity of former times in this Church and State, under the present government of the Church.

Yet, by a strange fatality, these men suffer, either by

their absence, or silence, or negligence, or supine credulity (believing that all is good which is gilded with shows of zeal and reformation), their private dissenting in judgment to be drawn into the common sewer or stream of the present vogue and humour; which hath its chief rise and abetment from those popular clamours and tumults, which served to give life and strength to the infinite activity of those men who studied with all diligence and policy to improve to their innovating designs the present distractions.

Such armies of Propositions having so little, in my judgment, of reason, justice, and religion, on their side, as they had tumult and faction for their rise, must not go alone, but ever be backed and seconded with armies of soldiers. Though the second should prevail against my person, yet the first shall never overcome me, further than I see cause; for I look not at their number and power so much as I weigh their reason and justice.

Had the two Houses first sued out their livery, and once effectually redeemed themselves from the wardship of the tumults (which can be no other than the hounds that attend the cry and holloa of those men who hunt after factious and private designs, to the ruin of Church and State); did my judgment tell me that the Propositions sent to me were the results of the major part of their votes, who exercise their freedom, as well as they have a right to sit in Parliament, I should then suspect my own judgment for not speedily and fully concurring with every one of them.

For I have charity enough to think there are wise men among them, and humility to think that, as in some things I may want, so it is fit I should use, their advice, which is the end for which I called them to a Parliament. But yet I cannot allow their wisdom such a completeness and inerrability as to exclude myself, since none of them hath that part to act, that trust to discharge, nor that estate and honour to preserve, as myself; without whose reason concurrent with theirs (as the sun's influence is necessary in all nature's productions), they cannot beget or bring forth any one complete and authoritative act of public wisdom, which makes the laws.

But the unreasonableness of some Propositions is not more evident to me than this is, that they are not the joint and free desires of those in their major number, who are of right to sit and vote in Parliament.

For many of them savour very strong of that old leaven of innovations, masked under the name of reformation, which in my two last famous predecessors' days heaved at, and sometime threatened, both Prince and Parliaments; but, I am sure, was never wont so far to infect the whole mass of the nobility and gentry of this kingdom, however it dispersed among the vulgar. Nor was it likely so suddenly to taint the major part of both Houses as that they should unanimously desire and affect so enormous and dangerous innovations in Church and State, contrary to their former education, practice, and judgment.

Not that I am ignorant how the choice of many

members was carried by much faction in the countries, some thirsting after nothing more than a passionate revenge of whatever displeasure they had conceived against me, my court, or the clergy.

But all reason bids me impute these sudden and vast desires of change to those few who armed themselves with the many-headed and many-handed tumults.

No less doth reason, honour, and safety, both of Church and State, command me to chew such morsels before I let them down. If the straitness of my conscience will not give me leave to swallow down such camels as others do of sacrilege and injustice both to God and man, they have no more cause to quarrel with me than for this, that my throat is not so wide as theirs. Yet by God's help I am resolved that nothing of passion, or peevishness, or list to contradict, or vanity to shew my negative power, shall have any bias upon my judgment to make me gratify my will, by denying anything which my reason and conscience commands me not.

Nor, on the other side, will I consent to more than reason, justice, honour, and religion persuade me to be for God's glory, the Church's good, my people's welfare, and my own peace.

I will study to satisfy my Parliament and my people, but I will never, for fear or flattery, gratify any faction, how potent soever, for this were to nourish the disease and oppress the body.

Although many men's loyalty and prudence are terrified from giving me that free and faithful counsel which they are able and willing to impart, and I may want, yet none can hinder me from craving of the counsel of that mighty Counsellor, who can both suggest what is best, and incline my heart stedfastly to follow it.

O Thou first and eternal Reason, whose wisdom is fortified with omnipotency, furnish Thy servant first with clear discoveries of truth, reason, and justice in my understanding; then so confirm my will and resolution to adhere to them, that no terrors, injuries, or oppressions of my enemies may ever enforce me against those rules which Thou by them hast planted in my conscience.

Thou never madest me a king that I should be less than a man, and not dare to say yea or nay, as I see cause; which freedom is not denied to the meanest creature that hath the use of reason and liberty of speech.

Shall that be blameable in me, which is commendable veracity and constancy in others?

Thou seest, O Lord, with what partiality and injustice they deny that freedom to me their King which Thou hast given to all men, and which themselves pertinaciously challenge to themselves, while they are so tender of the least breach of their privileges.

To Thee I make my supplication, who canst guide us by an unerring rule through the perplexed labyrinths of our own thoughts and other men's proposals, which I have some cause to suspect are purposely cast as snares, that by my granting or denying them I might be more entangled in those difficulties wherewith they lie in wait to afflict me.

O Lord, make Thy way plain before me.

Let not my own sinful passions cloud or divert Thy sacred suggestions.

Let Thy glory be my end, Thy Word my rule, and then Thy will be done.

I cannot please all, I care not to please some men. If I may be happy to please Thee I need not fear whom I displease.

Thou that makest the wisdom of the world foolishness, and takest in their own devices such as are wise in their own conceits, make me wise by Thy truth, for Thy honour, my kingdom's general good, and my own soul's salvation, and I shall not much regard the world's opinion or diminution of me.

The less wisdom they are willing to impute to me, the more they shall be convinced of Thy wisdom directing me, while I deny nothing fit to be granted, out of crossness or humour, nor grant anything which is to be denied, out of any fear or flattery of men.

Suffer me not to be guilty or unhappy by willing or inconsiderate advancing any men's designs which are injurious to the public good, while I confirm them by my consent.

Nor let me be any occasion to hinder or defraud the public of what is best, by any morose or perverse dissentings.

Make me so humbly charitable as to follow their advice when it appears to be for the public good, of whose affections to me I have yet but few evidences to assure me.

Thou canst as well bless honest errors, as blast fraudulent counsels.

Since we must give an account of every evil and idle word in private at Thy tribunal, Lord, make me careful *of those solemn declarations of my mind which are like to have the greatest influence upon the public, either for woe or weal.*

The less others consider what they ask, make me the more solicitous what I answer.

Though mine own and my people's pressures are grievous, and peace would be very pleasing, yet, Lord, never suffer me to avoid the one or purchase the other with the least expense or waste of my conscience, whereof Thou, O Lord, only are deservedly more master than myself.

XII.

UPON THE REBELLION AND TROUBLES IN IRELAND.

THE commotions in Ireland were so sudden and so violent, that it was hard at first either to discern the rise or apply a remedy to that precipitant rebellion.

Indeed, that sea of blood which hath there been cruelly and barbarously shed, is enough to drown any man in eternal both infamy and misery, whom God shall find the malicious author or instigator of its effusion.

It fell out, as a most unhappy advantage to some men's malice against me, that when they had impudence enough to lay anything to my charge, this bloody opportunity should be offered them, with which I must be aspersed, although there was nothing which could be more abhorred by me, being so full of sin against God, disloyalty to myself, and destructive to my subjects.

Some men took it very ill not to be believed when they affirmed that what the Irish rebels did was done with my privity at least, if not by my commission. But these knew too well that it is no news for some of my subjects to fight, not only without my commission, but against my command and person too, yet all the while to pretend they fight by my authority and for my safety.

I would to God the Irish had nothing to allege for their imitation against those whose blame must needs be the greater, by how much Protestant principles are more against all rebellion against princes than those of Papists. Nor will the goodness of men's intentions excuse the scandal and contagion of their examples.

But whoever fail of their duty toward me, I must bear the blame. This honour my enemies have always done to me, to think moderate injuries not proportionate to me, nor competent trials either of my patience under them, or my pardon of them.

Therefore with exquisite malice they have mixed the gall and vinegar of falsity and contempt with the cup of my affliction, charging me not only with untruths, but such as wherein I have the greatest share of loss and dishonour by what is committed; whereby (in all policy, reason, and religion, having least cause to give the least consent, and most grounds of utter detestation) I might be represented by them to the world the more inhuman and barbarous; like some Cyclopic monster, whom nothing will serve to eat and drink but the flesh and blood of my own subjects, in whose common welfare my interest lies as much as some men's doth in their perturbations, who think they cannot do well but in evil times, nor so cunningly, as in laying the odium of those sad events on others, wherewith themselves are most pleased, and whereof they have been not the least occasion.

And certainly, it is thought by many wise men that the preposterous rigour and unreasonable severity which some men carried before them in England, was not the least incentive that kindled and blew up into those horrid flames the sparks of discontent; which wanted not predisposed fuel for rebellion in Ireland, where despair being added to their former discontents, and the fears of utter extirpation to their wonted oppressions, it was easy to provoke to an open rebellion. People prone enough to break out to all exorbitant violence, both by some principles of their religion, and the natural desires of liberty, both to exempt themselves from their present restraints, and to prevent those after rigours wherewith they saw themselves apparently threatened by the covetous zeal and uncharitable fury of some men, who think it a great argument of the truth of their religion to endure no other but their own.

God knows, as I can with truth wash my hands in innocency as to any guilt in that rebellion, so I might wash them in my tears as to the sad apprehensions I had to see it spread so far, and make such waste; and this in a time when distractions and jealousies here in England made most men rather intent to their own safety, or designs they were driving, than to the relief of those who were every day inhumanly butchered in

Ireland, whose tears and blood might, if nothing else, have quenched, or at least for a time repressed and smothered, those sparks of civil dissensions and jealousies which in England some men most industriously scattered.

I would to God no man had been less affected with Ireland's sad estate than myself. I offered to go myself in person upon that expedition, but some men were either afraid I should have any one kingdom quieted, or loth they were to shoot at any mark here less than myself, or that any should have the glory of my destruction but themselves. Had my many offers been accepted, I am confident neither the ruin had been so great, nor the calamity so long, nor the remedy so desperate.

So that, next to the sin of those who began that rebellion, theirs must needs be, who either hindered the speedy suppressing of it by domestic dissensions, or diverted the aids, or exasperated the rebels to the most desperate resolutions and actions, by threatening all extremities, not only to the known heads and chief incendiaries, but even to the whole community of that nation; resolving to destroy root and branch, men, women, and children, without any regard to those usual pleas for mercy, which conquerors, not wholly barbarous, are wont to hear from their own breasts in behalf of those whose oppressive fears, rather than their malice, engaged them; or whose imbecility for sex and age was such as they could neither lift up a hand against them, nor distinguish between their right hand and their left. Which preposterous, and, I think, unevangelical zeal, is too like that of the rebuked disciples, who would go no lower in their revenge than to call for fire from heaven for the repulse or neglect of a few; or like that of Jacob's sons, which the father both blamed and cursed, choosing rather to use all extremities which might drive men to desperate obstinacy, than to apply moderate remedies, such as might punish some with exemplary justice, yet disarm others, with tenders of mercy upon their submission, and our protection of them from the fury of those who would soon drown them if they refused to swim down the popular stream with them.

But some kind of zeal counts all merciful moderation lukewarmness, and had rather be cruel than counted cold, and is not seldom more greedy to kill the bear for his skin, than for any harm he hath done; the confiscation of men's estates being more beneficial than the charity of saving their lives or reforming their errors.

When all proportionable succours of the poor Protestants in Ireland (who were daily massacred and overborne with numbers of now desperate enemies) was diverted and obstructed here, I was earnestly entreated and generally advised by the chief of the Protestant party there to get them some respite and breathing by a cessation; without which they saw no probability, unless by a miracle, to preserve the remnant that had yet escaped. God knows with how much commiseration and solicitous caution I carried on that business by persons of honour and integrity, that so I might neither encourage the rebels' insolence, nor discourage the Protestants' loyalty and patience.

Yet when this was effected in the best sort that the necessity and difficulty of affairs would then permit, I was then to suffer again in my reputation and honour, because I suffered not the rebels utterly to devour the remaining handfuls of the Protestants there.

I thought that, in all reason, the gaining of that respite could not be so much to the rebels' advantages (which some have highly calumniated against me) as it might have been for the Protestants' future as well as present safety; if, during the time of that cessation, some men had had the grace to have laid Ireland's sad condition more to heart, and laid aside those violent motions which were here carried on by those that had better skill to let blood than to stanch it.

But in all the misconstructions of my actions (which are prone to find more credulity in men to what is false and evil, than love or charity to what is true and good), as I have no judge but God above me, so I can have comfort to appeal to His omniscience, who doth not therefore deny my innocence because he is pleased so far to try my patience, as He did His servant Job's.

I have enough to do to look to my own conscience and the faithful discharge of my trust as a king; I have scarce leisure to consider those swarms of reproaches which issue out of some men's mouths and hearts, as easily as smoke or sparks do out of a furnace, much less to make such prolix apologies as might give those men satisfaction, who, conscious to their own depth of wickedness, are loth to believe any man not to be as bad as themselves.

It is kingly to do well and hear ill. If I can but act the one, I shall not much regard to hear the other.

I thank God I can hear with patience as bad as my worst enemies can falsely say, and I hope I shall still do better than they desire or deserve I should.

I believe it will at last appear that they who first began to embroil my other kingdoms, are in great part guilty, if not of the first letting out, yet of the not timely stopping, those horrid effusions of blood in Ireland.

Which, whatever my enemies please to say or think, I look upon, as that of my other kingdoms, exhausted out of my own veins, no man being so much weakened by it as myself. And I hope, though men's unsatiable cruelties never will, yet the mercy of God will at length say to His justice, "It is enough," and command the sword of civil wars to sheath itself; His merciful justice intending, I trust, not our utter confusion, but our cure; the abatement of our sins, not the desolating of these nations.

O my God, let those infinite mercies prevent us once again, which I and my kingdoms have formerly abused, and can never deserve should be restored.

Thou seest how much cruelty among Christians is acted under the colour of religion, as if we could not be Christians unless we crucify one another.

Because we have not more loved Thy truth, and practised in charity, Thou hast suffered a spirit of error and bitterness, of mutual and mortal hatred, to arise among us.

O Lord, forgive wherein we have sinned, and sanctify what we have suffered.

Let our repentance be our recovery, as our great sins have been our ruin.

Let not the miseries I and my kingdoms have hitherto suffered seem small to Thee, but make our sins appear to our consciences as they are represented in the glass of Thy judgments; for Thou never punishest small failings with so severe afflictions.

O therefore, according to the multitude of Thy great mercies, pardon our sins, and remove Thy judgments, which are very many and very heavy.

Yet, let our sins be evermore grievous to us than Thy judgments, and make us more willing to repent than to be relieved. First give us the peace of penitent consciences, and then the tranquility of united kingdoms.

In the sea of our Saviour's blood drown our sins; and through this Red Sea of our own blood bring us at last to a state of piety, peace, and plenty.

As my public relations to all make me share in all my subjects' sufferings, so give me such a pious sense of them as becomes a Christian King and a loving Father of my people.

Let the scandalous and unjust reproaches cast upon me be as a breath more to kindle my compassion. Give me grace to heap charitable coals of fire upon their heads to melt them, whose malice or cruel zeal hath kindled, or hindered the quenching of those flames which have so much wasted my three kingdoms.

O rescue and assist those poor Protestants in Ireland, whom Thou hast hitherto preserved.

And lead those in the ways of Thy saving truths whose ignorance or errors have filled them with rebellious and destructive principles, which they act under an opinion that they do Thee good service.

Let the hand of Thy justice be against those who maliciously and despitefully have raised or fomented those cruel and desperate wars.

Thou that art far from destroying the innocent with the guilty, and the erroneous with the malicious, Thou that hadst pity on Nineveh for the many children that were therein, give not over the whole stock of that populous and seduced nation to the wrath of those whose covetousness makes them cruel, nor to their anger, which is too fierce and therefore justly cursed.

Preserve, if it be Thy will, in the midst of the furnace of Thy severe justice, a posterity which may praise Thee for Thy mercy.

And deal with me not according to man's unjust reproaches, but according to the innocency of my hands in Thy sight.

If I have desired or delighted in the woful day of my kingdom's calamities, if I have not earnestly studied and faithfully endeavoured the preventing and composing of these bloody distractions, then let Thy hand be against me and my father's house. O Lord, thou seest I have enemies enough of men; as I need not so I should not dare thus to imprecate Thy curse on me and mine, if my conscience did not witness my integrity, which Thou, O

Lord, knowest right well. But I trust not to my own merit, but Thy mercies. Spare us, O Lord, and be not angry with us for ever.

XIII.

Upon the Calling in of the Scots, and their Coming.

The Scots are a nation upon whom I have not only common ties of nature, sovereignty and bounty, with my father of blessed memory, but also special and late obligations of favours, having gratified the active spirits among them so far, that I seemed to many to prefer the desires of that party before my own interest and honour. But, I see, royal bounty emboldens some men to ask and act beyond all bounds of modesty and gratitude.

My charity and act of pacification forbids me to reflect on former passages, wherein I shall ever be far from letting any man's ingratitude or inconstancy make me repent of what I granted them for the public good. I pray God it may so prove.

The coming again of that party into England with an army, only to conform this Church to their late new model, cannot but seem as unreasonable as they would have thought the same measure offered from hence to themselves.

Other errand I could never understand they had (besides those common and vulgar flourishes for religion and liberty), save only to confirm the Presbyterian copy they had set, by making this Church to write after them, though it were in bloody characters.

Which design and end, whether it will justify the use of such violent means before the divine justice, I leave to their consciences to judge, who have already felt the misery of the means, but not reaped the benefit of the end, either in this kingdom or that.

Such knots and crossness of grain being objected here, as will hardly suffer that form which they cry up as the only just reformation, and settling of government and discipline in Churches, to go on so smoothly here as it might do in Scotland; and was by them imagined would have done in England, when so many of the English Clergy, through levity or discontent, if no worse passion, suddenly quitted their former engagements to Episcopacy, and faced about to their Presbytery.

It cannot but seem either passion or some self-seeking, more than true zeal and pious discretion, for any foreign State or Church to prescribe such medicines only for others which themselves have used rather successfully than commendably, not considering that the same physic on different constitutions will have different operations, that may kill one which doth but cure another.

Nor do I know any such tough and malignant humours in the constitution of the English Church which gentler applications than those of an army might not easily have removed; nor is it so proper to hew out religious reformations by the sword, as to polish them by fair and equal disputations among those that are most concerned in the differences, whom not force but reason ought to convince.

But their design now seemed rather to cut off all disputation here, than to procure a fair and equal one; for it was concluded there that the English clergy must conform to the Scots pattern, before ever they could be heard what they could say for themselves, or against the others' way.

I could have wished fairer proceedings, both for their credits who urge things with such violence, and for other men's consciences too, who can receive little satisfaction in these points, which are maintained rather by soldiers fighting in the field, than scholars disputing in free and learned synods.

Sure, in matters of religion, those truths gain most on men's judgments and consciences which are least urged with secular violence, which weakens truth with prejudices, and is unreasonable to be used, till such means of rational conviction have been applied, as, leaving no excuse for ignorance, condemns men's obstinacy to deserved penalties.

Which no charity will easily suspect of so many learned and pious Churchmen in England, who being always bred up and conformable to the government of Episcopacy, cannot so soon renounce both their former opinion and practice only because that party of the Scots will needs by force assist a like party here, either to drive all ministers like sheep into the common fold of Presbytery, or destroy them, at least fleece them, by depriving them of the benefit of their flocks. If the Scotch sole Presbytery were proved to be the only institution of Jesus Christ for all Churches' government, yet I believe it would be hard to prove that Christ had given those Scots, or any other of my subjects, commission by the sword to set it up in any of my kingdoms without my consent.

What respect and obedience Christ and His Apostles paid to the chief governors of states where they lived, is very clear in the Gospel; but that He or they ever commanded to set up such a parity of Presbyters, and in such a way as those Scots endeavour, I think is not very disputable.

If Presbytery, in such a supremacy, be an institution of Christ, sure it differs from all others, and is the first and only point of Christianity that was to be planted and watered with so much Christian blood, whose effusions run in a stream so contrary to that of the primitive planters both of Christianity and Episcopacy, which was with patient shedding of their own blood, not violent drawing other men's. Sure there is too much of man in it to have much of Christ, none of whose institutions were carried on or begun with the temptations of covetousness or ambition, of both which this is vehemently suspected.

Yet was there never anything upon the point which those Scots had by army or commissioners to move me with, by their many solemn obtestations and pious threatenings, but only this, to represent to me the wonderful necessity of setting up their Presbytery in England to avoid the further miseries of a war, which some men chiefly on this design, at first had begun, and now further engaged themselves to continue.

What hinders that any sects, schisms, or heresies, if they can get but numbers, strength, and opportunity, may not, according to this opinion and pattern, set up their ways by the like methods of violence? All which Presbytery seeks to suppress, and render odious under those names; when wise and learned men think that nothing hath more marks of schism and sectarism than this Presbyterian way, both as to the ancient and still most universal way of the Church government, and specially as to the particular laws and constitutions of this English Church; which are not yet repealed, nor are like to be for me, till I see more rational and religious motives than soldiers use to carry in their knapsacks.

But we must leave the success of all to God, who hath many ways (having first taken us off from the folly of our opinions and fury of our passion) to teach us those rules of true reason and peaceable wisdom which is from above, tending most to God's glory and His Church's good; which I think myself so much the more bound in conscience to attend with the most judicious zeal and care, by how much I esteem the Church above the State, the glory of Christ above mine own, and the salvation of men's souls above the preservation of their bodies and estates.

Nor may any men, I think, without sin and presumption, forcibly endeavour to cast the Churches under my care and tuition into the moulds they have fancied and fashioned to their designs, till they have first gained my consent, and resolved both my own and other men's consciences by the strength of their reasons.

Other violent motions, which are neither manly, Christian, nor loyal, shall never either shake or settle my religion; nor any man's else who knows what religion means, and how far it is removed from all faction, whose proper engine is force, the arbitrator of beasts, not of reasonable men, much less of humble Christians and loyal subjects in matters of religion.

But men are prone to have such high conceits of themselves, that they care not what cost they lay out upon their opinions, especially those that have some temptations of gain to recompense their losses and hazards.

Yet I was not more scandalized at the Scots armies coming in against my will, and their forfeiture of so many obligations of duty and gratitude to me, that I wondered how those here could so much distrust God's assistance, who so much pretended God's cause to the people as if they had the certainty of some divine revelation, considering they were more than competently furnished with my subjects' arms and ammunition, my navy by sea, my forts, castles, and cities by land.

But I find that men, jealous of the justifiableness of their doings and designs before God, never think they have human strength enough to carry their work on, seem it never so plausible to the people. What cannot be justified in law or religion, had need be fortified with power.

And yet such is the inconstancy that attends all minds engaged in violent motion, that whom some of them one while earnestly invite to come in to their assistance, others of them soon after are weary of, and with nauseating cast them out; what one party thought to rivet to a settledness by the strength and influence of the Scots, that the other rejects and contemns; at once despising the Kirk government and discipline of the Scots, and frustrating the success of so chargeable, more than charitable, assistance. For sure the Church of England might have purchased at a far cheaper rate the truth and happiness of reformed government and discipline if it had been wanting, though it had entertained the best divines of Christendom for their advice in a full and free synod; which I was ever willing to, and desirous of, that matters being impartially settled might be more satisfactory to all and more durable.

But much of God's justice and man's folly will at length be discovered through all the films and pretensions of religion in which politicians wrap up their designs: in vain do men hope to build their piety on the ruins of loyalty. Nor can those confederations or designs be durable when subjects make bankrupt of their allegiance, under pretence of setting up a quicker trade for religion.

But as my best subjects of Scotland never deserted me, so I cannot think that the most are gone so far from me, in a prodigality of their love and respects towards me, as to make me to despair of their return; when, besides the bonds of nature and conscience which they have to me, all reason and true policy will teach them that their chiefest interest consists in their fidelity to the crown, not in their serviceableness to any party of the people, to a neglect and betraying of my safety and honour for their own advantages. However, the less cause I have to trust to men, the more I shall apply myself to God.

The troubles of my soul are enlarged; O Lord, bring Thou me out of my distress.

Lord, direct Thy servant in the ways of that pious simplicity, which is the best policy.

Deliver me from the combined strength of those, who have so much of the serpent's subtilty that they forget the dove's innocency.

Though hand join in hand, yet let them not prevail against my soul to the betraying of my conscience and honour.

Thou, O Lord, canst turn the hearts of those parties in both nations, as Thou didst the men of Judah and Israel to restore David with as much loyal zeal as they did with inconstancy and eagerness pursue him.

Preserve the love of Thy truth and uprightness in me, and I shall not despair of my subjects' affections returning towards me.

Thou canst soon cause the overflowing seas to ebb, and retire back again to the bounds which Thou hast appointed for them.

O my God, I trust in Thee; let me not be ashamed, let not my enemies triumph over me.

Let them be ashamed who transgress without a cause; let them be turned back that persecute my soul.

Let integrity and uprightness preserve me, for I wait on Thee, O Lord.

Redeem Thy Church, O God, out of all its troubles.

XIV.

Upon the Covenant.

The Presbyterian Scots are not to be hired at the ordinary rate of auxiliaries; nothing will induce them to engage till those that call them in have pawned their souls to them by a solemn league and covenant:

Where many engines of religious and fair pretensions are brought, chiefly to batter or raze Episcopacy. This they make the grand evil spirit, which, with some other imps purposely added to make it more odious and terrible to the vulgar, must by so solemn a charm and exorcism be cast out of this Church after more than a thousand years' possession here, from the first plantation of Christianity in this island, and an universal prescription of time and practice in all other Churches since the Apostles' times till this last century.

But no antiquity must plead for it: Presbytery, like a young heir, thinks the father hath lived long enough; and impatient not to be in the bishop's chair and authority (though laymen go away with the revenues), all art is used to sink Episcopacy, and launch Presbytery in England, which was lately buoyed up in Scotland by the like artifice of a Covenant.

Although I am unsatisfied with many passages in that Covenant (some referring to myself with very dubious and dangerous limitations,) yet I chiefly wonder at the design and drift touching the discipline and government of the Church; and such a manner of carrying them on to new ways by oaths and covenants, where it is hard for men to be engaged by no less than swearing for or against those things which are of no clear moral necessity, but very disputable, and controverted among learned and godly men, whereto the application of oaths can hardly be made and enjoined with that judgment and certainty in one's self, or that charity and candour to others of different opinion, as I think religion requires, which never refuses fair and equable deliberations, yea, and dissentings too in matters only probable.

The enjoining of oaths upon people must needs in things doubtful be dangerous, as in things unlawful, damnable; and no less superfluous where former religious and legal engagements bound men sufficiently to all necessary duties. Nor can I see how they will reconcile such an innovating oath and covenant with that former protestation which was so lately taken, to maintain the religion established in the Church of England, since they count discipline so great a part of religion.

But ambitious minds never think they have laid snares and gins enough to catch and hold the vulgar credulity, for by such politic and seemingly-pious stratagems they think to keep the populacy fast to their parties under the terror of perjury; whereas certainly all honest and wise men ever thought themselves sufficiently bound by former ties of religion, allegiance, and laws, to God and man.

Nor can such after-contracts, devised and imposed by a few men in a declared party, without my consent, and without any like power or precedent from God's or man's laws, be ever thought by judicious men sufficient either to absolve or slacken those moral and eternal bonds of duty which lie upon all my subjects' consciences, both to God and me.

Yet as things now stand, good men shall least offend God or me by keeping their covenant in honest and lawful ways, since I have the charity to think that the chief end of the covenant in such men's intentions was to preserve religion in purity and the kingdoms in peace: to other than such ends and means they cannot think themselves engaged. Nor will those that have any true touches of conscience endeavour to carry on the best designs (much less such as are, and will be daily more apparently factious and ambitious) by any unlawful means, under that title of the Covenant, unless they dare prefer ambiguous, dangerous, and unauthorized novelties before their known and sworn duties, which are indispensable, both to God and myself.

I am prone to believe and hope that many who took the Covenant are yet firm to this judgment, that such later vows, oaths, or leagues can never blot out those former gravings and characters which by just and lawful oaths were made upon their souls.

That which makes such confederations, by way of

solemn leagues and covenants, more to be suspected is, that they are the common road used in all factions and powerful perturbations of State or Church; where formalities of extraordinary zeal and piety are never more studied and elaborate than when politicians most agitate desperate designs against all that is settled or sacred in religion and laws, which by such screws are cunningly, yet forcibly, wrested by secret steps and less sensible degrees, from their known rule and wonted practice, to comply with the humours of those men who aim to subdue all to their own will and power, under the disguises of holy combinations.

Which cords and withes will hold men's consciences no longer than force attends and twists them; for every man soon grows his own pope, and easily absolves himself of those ties which, not the commands of God's word or the laws of the land, but only the subtilty and terror of a party casts upon him, either superfluous and vain when they were sufficiently tied before, or fraudulent and injurious, if by such after-ligaments they find the imposers really aiming to dissolve or suspend their former just and necessary obligations.

Indeed, such illegal ways seldom or never intend the engaging men more to duties, but only to parties; therefore it is not regarded how they keep their covenants in point of piety pretended, provided they adhere firmly to the party and design intended.

I see the imposers of it are content to make their Covenant like manna (not that it came from heaven as this did), agreeable to every man's palate and relish who will but swallow it. They admit any men's senses of it, though diverse or contrary, with any salvos, cautions, and reservations, so as they cross not their chief design, which is laid against the Church and me.

It is enough if they get but the reputation of a seeming increase to their party: so little do men remember that God is not mocked.

In such latitudes of sense I believe many that love me and the Church well may have taken the Covenant, who are yet so fondly and superstitiously taken by it as now to act clearly against both all piety and loyalty; who first yielded to it, more to prevent that imminent violence and ruin which hung over their heads, in case they wholly refused it, than for any value of it or devotion to it.

Wherein the latitude of some general clauses may perhaps serve somewhat to relieve them, as of *Doing and endeavouring what lawfully they may, in their places and callings,* and *according to the word of God.* For these, indeed, carry no man beyond those bounds of good conscience which are certain and fixed, either in God's laws as to the general, or the laws of the State and kingdom as to the particular, regulation and exercise of men's duties.

I would to God such as glory most in the name of Covenanters would keep themselves within those lawful bounds to which God hath called them. Surely it were the best way to expiate the rashness of taking it; which must needs then appear, when, besides the want of a full and lawful authority at first to enjoin it, it shall actually be carried on beyond and against those ends which were in it specified and pretended. I willingly forgive such men's taking the Covenant who keep it within such bounds of piety, law, and loyalty, as can never hurt either the Church, myself, or the public peace, against which no man's lawful calling can engage him.

As for that reformation of the Church which the Covenant pretends, I cannot think it just or comely that by the partial advice of a few divines (of so soft and servile tempers as disposed them to so sudden acting and compliance, contrary to their former judgments, profession and practice), such foul scandals and suspicions should be cast upon the doctrine and government of the Church of England as was never done (that I have heard) by any that deserved the name of reformed Churches abroad, nor by any men of learning and candour at home, all whose judgments I cannot but prefer before any men's now factiously engaged.

No man can be more forward than myself to carry on all due reformations with mature judgment and a good conscience, in what things I shall, after impartial advice, be by God's word and right reason convinced to be amiss. I have offered more than ever the fullest, freest, and wisest Parliaments did desire.

But the sequel of some men's actions makes it evident, that the main reformation intended is the abasing of Episcopacy into Presbytery, and the robbing the Church of its lands and revenues; for no men have been more injuriously used, as to their legal rights, than the bishops and Churchmen. These, as the fattest deer, must be destroyed; the other rascal herd of schisms, heresies, &c., being lean, may enjoy the benefit of a toleration. Thus Naboth's vineyard made him the only blasphemer of his city, and fit to die. Still, I see, while the breath of religion fills the sails, profit is the compass by which factious men steer their course in all seditious commotions.

I thank God, as no man lay more open to the sacrilegious temptation of usurping the Church's lands and revenues (which, issuing chiefly from the Crown, are held of it, and legally can revert only to the Crown with my consent), so I have always had such a perfect abhorrence of it in my soul, that I never found the least inclination to such sacrilegious reformings; yet no man hath a greater desire to have bishops and all Churchmen so reformed, that they may best deserve and use, not only what the pious munificence of my predecessors hath given to God and the Church, but all other additions of Christian bounty.

But no necessity shall ever, I hope, drive me or mine to invade or sell the priest's lands, which both Pharaoh's divinity and Joseph's true piety abhorred to do. So unjust I think it, both in the eye of reason and religion, to deprive the most sacred employment of all due encouragements, and like that other hardhearted Pharaoh, to withdraw the straw and increase the task; so pursuing the oppressed Church, as some have done, to the Red Sea of a civil war, where nothing but a miracle can save either it, or him who esteems it his greatest title to be called, and his chiefest glory to be, "The Defender of the Church, both in its true faith and its just fruitions, equally abhorring sacrilege and apostacy."

I had rather live, as my predecessor Henry the Third sometime did, on the Church's alms, than violently to take the bread out of the bishops' and ministers' mouths.

The next work will be Jeroboam's reformation, consecrating the meanest of the people to be priests in Israel, to serve those golden calves who have enriched themselves with the Church's patrimony and dowry, which how it thrived both with prince, priests, and people is well enough known. And so it will be here, when from the tutition of kings and queens which have been nursing fathers and mothers of this Church, it shall be at their allowance who have already discovered what hard fathers and stepmothers they will be.

If the poverty of Scotland might, yet the plenty of England cannot excuse the envy and rapine of the Church's rights and revenues.

I cannot so much as pray God to prevent those sad consequences which will inevitably follow the parity and poverty of ministers, both in Church and State; since I think it no less than a mocking and tempting of God to desire Him to hinder those mischiefs whose occasions and remedies are in our own power, it being every man's sin not to avoid the one and not to use the other.

There are ways enough to repair the breaches of the

State without the ruins of the Church. As I would be a restorer of the one, so I would not be an oppressor of the other under the pretence of public debts; the occasions contracting them were bad enough, but such a discharging of them would be much worse. I pray God neither I or mine may be accessory to either.

To Thee, O Lord, do I address my prayer, beseeching Thee to pardon the rashness of my subjects' swearings, and to quicken their sense and observation of those just, moral, and indispensable bonds which Thy word and the laws of this kingdom have laid upon their consciences, from which no pretensions of piety and reformation are sufficient to absolve them, or to engage them to any contrary practices.

Make them at length seriously to consider that nothing violent and injurious can be religious.

Thou allowest no man's committing sacrilege under the zeal of abhoring idols.

Suffer not sacrilegious designs to have the countenance of religious ties.

Thou hast taught us by the wisest of kings that it is a snare to take things that are holy, and after vows to make enquiry.

Ever keep Thy servant from consenting to perjurious and sacrilegious rapines, that I may not have the brand and curse to all posterity of robbing Thee and Thy Church of what Thy bounty hath given us, and Thy clemency hath accepted from us, wherewith to encourage learning and religion.

Though my treasures are exhausted, my revenues diminished, and my debts increased, yet never suffer me to be tempted to use such profane reparations, lest a coal from Thine altar set such a fire on my throne and conscience as will be hardly quenched.

Let not the debts and engagements of the public, which some men's folly and prodigality hath contracted, be an occasion to impoverish the Church.

The State may soon recover by Thy blessing and peace upon us, the Church is never likely in times where the charity of most men is grown so cold, and their religion so illiberal.

Continue to those that serve Thee and Thy Church all those encouragements which by the will of the pious donors and the justice of the laws are due unto them; and give them grace to deserve and use them aright to Thy glory and the relief of the poor, that Thy priests may be clothed with righteousness, and the poor may be satisfied with bread.

Let not holy things be given to swine, nor the Church's bread to dogs; rather let them go about the city, grin like a dog, and grudge that they are not satisfied.

Let those sacred morsels, which some men have already by violence devoured, never digest with them nor theirs; let them be as Naboth's vineyard to Ahab, gall in their mouths, rottenness to their names, a moth to their families, and a sting to their consciences.

Break in sunder, O Lord, all violent and sacrilegious confederations to do wickedly and injuriously.

Divide their hearts and tongues who have banded together

against the Church and State, that the folly of such may be manifest to all men, and proceed no farther.

But so favour my righteous dealing, O Lord, that in the mercies of Thee, the Most High, I may never miscarry.

XV.

Upon the many Jealousies raised, and Scandals cast upon the King, to stir up the People against him.

If I had not my own innocency and God's protection, it were hard for me to stand out against those stratagems and conflicts of malice which by falsities seek to oppress the truth, and by jealousies to supply the defect of real causes, which might seem to justify so unjust engagements against me.

And, indeed, the worst effects of open hostility come short of these designs; for I can more willingly lose my crowns than my credit, nor are my kingdoms so dear to me as my reputation and honour.

Those must have a period with my life; but these may survive to a glorious kind of immortality when I am dead and gone, a good name being the embalming of princes, and a sweet consecrating of them to an eternity of love and gratitude among posterity.

Those foul and false aspirations were secret engines at first employed against my people's love of me; that, undermining their opinion and value of me, my enemies, and theirs too, might at once blow up their affections and batter down their loyalty.

Wherein yet, I thank God, the detriment of my honour is not so afflictive to me as the sin and danger of my people's souls, whose eyes once blinded with such mists of suspicions, they are soon misled into the most desperate precipices of actions; wherein they do not only not consider their sin and danger, but glory in their zealous adventures, while I am rendered to them so fit to be destroyed, that many are ambitious to merit the name of my destroyers, imagining they then fear God most when they least honour their King.

I thank God I never found but my pity was above my anger; nor have my passions ever so prevailed against me as to exclude my most compassionate prayers for them, whom devout errors, more than their own malice, have betrayed to a most religious rebellion.

I had the charity to interpret that most part of my subjects fought against my supposed errors; not my person, and intended to mend me, not to end me. And I hope that God, pardoning their errors, hath so far accepted and answered their good intentions, that as He has yet preserved me, so He hath by these afflictions prepared me both to do Him better service and my people more good than hitherto I have done.

I do not more willingly forgive their seductions, which occasioned their loyal injuries, than I am ambitious by all princely merits to redeem them from their unjust suspicions, and reward them for their good intentions.

I am too conscious to my own affections toward the generality of my people, to suspect theirs to me; nor shall the malice of my enemies ever be able to deprive me of the comfort which that confidence gives me. I shall never gratify the spitefulness of a few, with any sinister thoughts of all their allegiance, whom pious frauds have seduced.

The worst some men's ambition can do shall never persuade me to make so bad interpretations of most of my subjects' actions, who possibly may be erroneous, but not heretical in point of loyalty.

The sense of the injuries done by my subjects is as sharp as those done to myself, our welfares being inseparable. In this only they suffer more than myself, that they are animated by some seducers to injure at once both themselves and me.

For this is not enough to the malice of my enemies that I be afflicted, but it must be done by such instruments, that my afflictions grieve me not more than this doth, that I am afflicted by those whose prosperity I earnestly desire, and whose seduction I heartily deplore.

If they had been my open and foreign enemies I could have borne it, but they must be my own subjects, who are, next to my children, dear to me, and for the restoring of whose tranquility I could willingly be the Jonah; if I did not evidently foresee that by the divided interests of their and mine enemies, as by contrary winds, the storm of their miseries would be rather increased than allayed.

I had rather prevent my people's ruin than rule over them; nor am I so ambitious of that dominion which is but my right, as of their happiness, if it could expiate or countervail such a way of obtaining it by the highest injuries of subjects committed against their sovereign.

Yet I had rather suffer all the miseries of life, and die many deaths, than shamefully to desert or dishonourably to betray my own just rights and sovereignty, thereby to gratify the ambition or justify the malice of my enemies; between whose malice and other men's mistakes I put as great a difference as between an ordinary ague and the plague, or the itch of novelty and the leprosy of disloyalty.

As liars need have good memories, so malicious persons need good inventions, that their calumnies may fit every man's fancy; and what their reproaches want of truth, they may make up with number and show.

My patience, I thank God, will better serve me to bear, and my charity to forgive, than my leisure to answer the many false aspirations which some men have cast upon me.

Did I not more consider my subjects' satisfaction than my own vindication, I should never have given the malice of some men that pleasure as to see me take notice of, or remember what they say or object.

I would leave the authors to be punished by their own evil manners and seared consciences, which will, I believe, in a shorter time than they be aware of, both confute and revenge all those black and false scandals which they have cast on me; and make the world see there is as little truth in them as there was little worth in the broaching of them, or civility, (I need not say loyalty) in the not suppressing of them: whose credit and reputation, even with the people, shall ere long be quite blasted by the breath of that same furnace of popular obloquy and detraction which they have studied to heat and inflame to the highest degree of infamy, and wherein they have sought to cast and consume my name and honour.

First, nothing gave me more cause to suspect and search my own innocency than when I observed so many forward to engage against me who had made great professions of singular piety; for this gave to vulgar minds so bad a reflection upon me and my cause as if it had been impossible to adhere to me, and not withal depart from God; to think or speak well of me, and not to blaspheme Him: so many were persuaded that these two were utterly inconsistent to be at once loyal to me and truly religious toward God.

Not but that I had, I thank God, many with me which were both learned and religious (much above that ordinary size and that vulgar proportion wherein some men glory so much,) who were so well satisfied in the cause of my sufferings, that they chose rather to suffer with me, than forsake me.

Nor is it strange that so religious pretensions as were used against me should be to many well-minded men a great temptation to oppose me; especially being urged by such popular preachers as think it no sin to lie for God, and what they please to call God's cause, cursing all that will not curse with them; looking so much at and crying up the goodness of the end propounded, that they consider not the lawfulness of the means used not the depth of the mischief chiefly plotted and intended.

The weakness of these men's judgments must be made up by their clamours and activity.

It was a great part of some men's religion to scandalize me and mine; they thought theirs could not be true if they cried not down mine as false.

I thank God I have had more trial of His grace, as to the constancy of my religion in the Protestant profession of the Church of England, both abroad and at home, than ever they are like to have.

Nor do I know any exception I am so liable to in their opinion as too great a fixedness in that religion whose judicious and solid grounds, both from Scripture and antiquity, will not give my conscience leave to approve or consent to those many dangerous and divided innovations, which the bold ignorance of some men would needs obtrude upon me and my people.

Contrary to those well-tried foundations both of truth and order, which men of far greater learning and clearer zeal have settled in the confession and constitution of this Church in England, which many former Parliaments, in the most calm and unpassionate times, have oft confirmed; in which I shall ever, by God's help, persevere, as believing it hath most of primitive truth and order.

Nor did my using the assistance of some Papists, which were my subjects, any way fight against my religion, as some men would needs interpret it; especially those who least of all men cared whom they employed, or what they said and did, so they might prevail.

It is strange that so wise men as they would be esteemed, should not conceive that differences of persuasion in matters of religion may easily fall out where there is the sameness of duty, allegiance, and subjection. The first they owe, as men and Christians to God; the second they owe to me in common, as their King. Different professions in point of religion cannot, any more than in civil trades, take away the community of relations, either to parents or to princes. And where is there such an olio or medley of various religions in the world again, as those men entertain in their service (who find most fault with me,) without any scruple, as to the diversity of their sects and opinions?

It was indeed a foul and indelible shame for such as would be counted Protestants to inforce me, a declared Protestant, their lord and King, to necessary use of Papists, or any other, who did but their duty to help me to defend myself.

Nor did I more than is lawful for any king, in such exigents, to use the aid of any of his subjects.

I am sorry the Papists should have a greater sense of their allegiance than many Protestant professors, who seem to have learned and to practise the worst principles of the worst Papists.

Indeed it had been a very impertinent and unseasonable scruple in me, and very pleasing, no doubt, to my enemies, to have been then disputing the points of different beliefs in by subjects when I was disputed with by swords' points, and when I needed the help of my subjects as men, no less than their prayers as Christians.

The noise of my evil counsellors was another useful device for those who were impatient any men's counsels but their own should be followed in Church or State, who were so eager in giving me better counsel that they would not give me leave to take it with freedom, as a man, or honour as a King; making their counsels more like a drench, that must be poured down, than a draught, which might be fairly and leisurely drunk if I liked it.

I will not justify beyond human errors and frailties myself or my counsellors: they might be subject to some miscarriages, yet such as were far more reparable by second and better thoughts than those enormous extravagances wherewith some men have now even wildered and almost quite lost both Church and State.

The event of things at last will make it evident to my subjects, that had I followed the worst counsels that my worst counsellors ever had the boldness to offer to me, or myself an inclination to use, I could not so soon have brought both Church and State in three flourishing kingdoms to such a chaos of confusions and hell of miseries as some have done; out of which they cannot, or will not, in the midst of their many great advantages, redeem either me or my subjects.

No men were more willing to complain than I was to redress what I saw in reason was either done or advised amiss; and this I thought I had done even beyond the expectation of moderate men, who were sorry to see me prone even to injure myself out of a zeal to relieve my subjects.

But other men's insatiable desire of revenge upon me, my court, and my clergy hath wholly beguiled both Church and State of the benefit of all my either retractations or concessions, and withal hath deprived all those (now so zealous persecutors) both of the comfort and reward of their former pretended persecutions, wherein they so much gloried among the vulgar, and which, indeed, a truly humble Christian will so highly prize as rather not to be relieved than to be revenged, so as to be bereaved of that crown of Christian patience which attends humble and injured sufferers.

Another artifice used to withdraw my people's affections from me to their designs was the noise and ostentation of liberty, which men are not more prone to desire than unapt to bear in the popular sense, which is to do what every man liketh best.

If the divinest liberty be to will what men should, and to do what they so will, according to reason, laws, and religion, I envy not my subjects that liberty which is all I desire to enjoy myself; so far am I from the desire of oppressing theirs. Nor were those lords and gentlemen which assisted me so prodigal of their liberties, as with their lives and fortunes to help on the enslaving of themselves and their posterities.

As to civil immunities, none but such as desire to drive on their ambitious and covetous designs over the ruins of Church and State, prince, peers, and people, will ever desire greater freedoms than the laws allow; whose bounds good men count their ornament and protection, others their manacles and oppression.

Nor is it just any man should expect the reward and benefit of the law, who despiseth its rule and direction, losing justly his safety, while he seeks an unreasonable liberty.

Time will best inform my subjects, that those are the best preservers of their true liberties who allow themselves the least licentiousness against or beyond the laws.

They will feel it at last to their cost, that it is impossible those men should be really tender of their fellow-subjects' liberties, who have the hardiness to use their king with so severe restraints, against all laws, both divine and human; under which yet I will rather perish, than complain to those who want nothing to complete their mirth and triumph, but such music.

In point of true conscientious tenderness (attended with humility and meekness, not with proud and arrogant activity, which seeks to hatch every egg of different opinion to a faction or schism), I have oft declared how little I desire my laws and sceptre should intrench on God's sovereignty, which is the only king of men's consciences; and yet He hath laid such restraints upon men, as commands them to be subject for conscience sake, giving no men liberty to break the law established further than with meekness and patience they are content to suffer the penalties annexed, rather than perturb the public peace.

The truth is, some men's thirst after novelties, others' despair to relieve the necessities of their fortunes, or satisfy their ambition in peaceable times, (distrusting God's providence as well as their own merits,) were the secret, but principal, impulsives to these popular commotions, by which subjects have been persuaded to expend much of those plentiful estates they got and enjoyed under my government in peaceable times; which yet must now be blasted with all the odious reproaches which impotent malice can invent, and myself exposed to all those contempts which may most diminish the majesty of a king, and increase the ungrateful insolences of my people.

For mine honour, I am well assured that as mine innocency is clear before God in point of any calumnies they object, so my reputation shall, like the sun, (after owls and bats have had their freedom in the night and darker times,) rise and recover itself to such a degree of splendour, as those feral birds shall be grieved to behold and unable to bear. For never were any princes more glorious, than those whom God hath suffered to be tried in the furnace of afflictions by their injurious subjects.

And who knows but the just and merciful God will do me good for some men's hard, false, and evil speeches against me? wherein they speak rather what they wish, than what they believe or know.

Nor can I suffer so much in point of honour by those rude and scandalous pamphlets (which, like fire in great conflagrations, fly up and down to set all places on like flames) as those men do, who, pretending to so much piety, are so forgetful of their duty to God and me; by no way ever vindicating the majesty of their King against any of those who, contrary to the precept of God and precedent of angels, *speak evil of dignities, and bring railing accusations against* those who are honoured with the name of *gods*.

But it is no wonder if men, not fearing God, should not honour their King.

They will easily contemn such shadows of God, who reverence not that supreme and adorable Majesty, in comparison of whom all the glory of men and angels is but obscurity; yet hath he graven such characters of divine authority and sacred power upon kings, as none may without sin seek to blot them out. Nor shall their black veils be able to hide the shining of my face while God gives me a heart frequently and humbly to converse with Him, from whom alone are all the irradiations of true glory and majesty.

Thou, O Lord, knowest my reproach and my dishonour; my adversaries are all before Thee.

My soul is among lions, among them that are set on fire, even the sons of men, whose teeth are spears and arrows, their tongue a sharp sword.

Mine enemies reproach me all the day long, and those that are mad against me are sworn together.

O my God, how long shall the sons of men turn my glory into shame? How long shall they love vanity, and seek after lies?

Thou hast heard the reproaches of wicked men on every side. Hold not Thy peace, lest my enemies prevail against me, and lay mine honour in the dust.

Thou, O Lord, shalt destroy them that speak lies; the Lord will abhor both the bloodthirsty and deceitful men.

Make my righteousness to appear as the light, and mine innocency to shine forth as the sun at noonday.

Suffer not my silence to betray mine innocency, nor my displeasure my patience; that after my Saviour's example, being reviled, I may not revile again, and being cursed by them, I may bless them.

Thou that wouldest not suffer Shimei's tongue to go unpunished, when by Thy judgments on David he might seem to justify his disdainful reproaches, give me grace to intercede with Thy mercy for these my enemies, that the reward of false and lying tongues, even hot burning coals of eternal fire, may not be brought upon them.

Let my prayers and patience be as water to cool and quench their tongues, who are already set on fire with the fire of hell, and tormented with those malicious flames.

Let me be happy to refute and put to silence their evil-speaking by well-doing; and let them enjoy not the fruit of their lips, but of my prayer for their repentance and Thy pardon.

Teach me David's patience, and Hezekiah's devotion, that I may look to Thy mercy through man's malice, and see Thy justice in their sin.

Let Sheba's seditious speeches, Rabshakeh's railing, and Shimei's cursing, provoke, as my humble prayer to Thee, so Thy renewed blessing toward me.

Though they curse, do Thou bless, and I shall be blessed, and make a blessing to my people:

That the stone which some builders refuse, may become the head-stone of the corner.

Look down from heaven and save me from the reproach of them that would swallow me up.

Hide me in the secret of Thy presence from the pride of man, and keep me from the strife of tongues.

XVI.

Upon the Ordinance against the Common Prayer-book.

It is no news to have all invocations ushered in with the name of reformations in Church and State by those who, seeking to gain reputation with the vulgar for their extraordinary parts and piety, must needs undo whatever was formerly settled never so well and wisely.

So hardly can the pride of those that study novelties allow former times any share or degree of wisdom or godliness.

And because matter of prayer and devotion to God justly bears a great part in religion (being the soul's more immediate converse with the Divine Majesty,) nothing could be more plausible to the people than to tell them they served God amiss in that point.

Hence our public Liturgy, or forms of constant prayers, must be (not amended, in what upon free and public advice might seem to sober men inconvenient for matter or manner, to which I should easily consent, but) wholly cashiered and abolished. And after many popular contempts offered to the book and those that used it according to their consciences and the laws in force, it must be crucified by an ordinance, the better to please either those men who gloried in their extemporary vein and fluency, or others who, conscious to their own formality in the use of it, thought they fully expiated the sin of not using it aright by laying all the blame upon it, and a total rejecting it as a dead letter, thereby to excuse the deadness of their hearts.

As for the matter contained in the book, sober and learned men have sufficiently vindicated it against the cavils and exceptions of those who thought it a part of piety to make what profane objections they could against it, especially for popery and superstition; whereas, no doubt, the Liturgy was exactly conformed to the doctrine of the Church of England, and this by all reformed Churches is confessed to be most sound and orthodox.

For the manner of using set and prescribed forms, there is no doubt but that wholesome words, being known and fitted to men's understandings, are soonest received into their hearts, and aptest to excite and carry along with them judicious and fervent affections.

Nor do I see any reason why Christians should be weary of a well-composed Liturgy (as I hold this to be) more than of all other things, wherein the constancy abates nothing of the excellency and usefulness.

I could never see any reason why any Christian should abhor, or be forbidden to use, the same forms of prayer, since he prays to the same God, believes in the same Saviour, professeth the same truths, reads the same Scriptures, hath the same duties upon him, and feels the same daily wants for the most part, both inward and outward, which are common to the whole Church.

Sure we may as well beforehand know what we pray as to whom we pray, and in what words as to what sense; when we desire the same things, what hinders we may not use the same words? Our appetite and digestion, too, may be good, when we use, as we pray for, *our daily bread.*

Some men, I hear, are so impatient not to use in all their devotions their own invention and gifts, that they not only disuse (as too many) but wholly cast away and contemn the Lord's Prayer; whose great guilt is, that it is the warrant and original pattern of all set liturgies in the Christian Church.

I ever thought that the proud ostentation of men's abilities for invention, and the vain affectations of variety for expressions in public prayer, or any sacred administrations, merits a greater brand of sin than that which they call coldness and barrenness. Nor are men in those novelties less subject to formal and superficial tempers (as to their hearts) than in the use of constant forms, where not the words but men's hearts are to blame.

I make no doubt but a man may be very formal in the most extemporary variety, and very fervently devout in the most wonted expressions. Nor is God more a

God of variety than of constancy; nor are constant forms of prayer more likely to flat and hinder the spirit of prayer and devotion, than unpremeditated and confused variety to distract and lose it.

Though I am not against a grave, modest, discreet, and humble use of ministers' gifts even in public, the better to fit and excite their own and the people's affections to the present occasions, yet I know no necessity why private and single abilities should quite justle out and deprive the Church of the joint abilities and concurrent gifts of many learned and godly men, such as the composers of the Service-book were, who may in all reason be thought to have more of gifts and graces enabling them to compose, with serious deliberation and concurrent advice, such forms of prayers as may best fit the Church's common wants, inform the hearers' understanding, and stir up that fiduciary and fervent application of their spirits (wherein consists the very life and soul of prayer, and that so much pretended spirit of prayer) than any private man by his solitary abilities can be presumed to have; which what they are many times (even there where they make a great noise and show) the affectations, emptiness, impertinency, rudeness, confusions, flattery, levity, obscurity, vain, and ridiculous repetitions, the senseless and ofttimes blasphemous expressions, all these burdened with a most tedious and intolerable length, do sufficiently convince all men but those who glory in that Pharisaic way.

Wherein men must be strangely impudent, and flatterers of themselves, not to have an infinite shame of what they so do and say in things of so sacred a nature, before God and the Church, after so ridiculous, and, indeed, profane a manner.

Nor can it be expected but that in duties of frequent performance, as sacramental administrations and the like, which are still the same, ministers must either come to use their own forms constantly, which are not like to be so sound or comprehensive of the nature of the duty as forms of public composure; or else they must every time affect new expressions when the subject is the same; which can hardly be presumed in any man's greatest sufficiencies, not to want (many times) much of that completeness, order, and gravity becoming those duties, which by this means are exposed at every celebration to every minister's private infirmities, indispositions, errors, disorders, and defects, both for judgment and expression.

A serious sense of which inconveniences in the Church unavoidably following every man's several manner of officiating, no doubt, first occasioned the wisdom and piety of the ancient Churches to remedy those mischiefs by the use of constant liturgies of public composure.

The want of which, I believe, this Church will sufficiently feel when the unhappy fruits of many men's ungoverned ignorance and confident defects shall be discovered in more errors, schisms, disorders, and uncharitable distractions in religion, which are already but too many, the more is the pity.

However, if violence must needs bring in and abet those innovations (that men may not seem to have nothing to do) which law, reason, and religion forbids at least to be so obtruded, as wholly to justle out the public Liturgy:

Yet nothing can excuse that most unjust and partial severity of those men, who either lately had subscribed to, used and maintained the Service-book; or refusing to use it, cried out of the rigour of the laws and bishops, which suffered them not to use the liberty of their consciences in not using it.

That these men, I say, should so suddenly change the Liturgy into a Directory, as if the spirit needed help for invention, though not for expressions; or as if matter prescribed did not as much stint and obstruct the spirit, as if it were clothed in and confined to fit words: (so slight and easy is that legerdemain which will serve to delude the vulgar.)

That further, they should use such severity as not to suffer, without penalty, any to use the Common Prayer-book publicly, although their consciences bind them to it as a duty of piety to God and obedience to the laws.

Thus I see no men are prone to be greater tyrants, and more rigorous exactors upon others to conform to their illegal novelties, than such whose pride was formerly least disposed to the obedience of lawful constitutions, and whose licentious humours most pretended conscientious liberties; which freedom with much regret they now allow to me and my chaplains, when they may have leave to serve me, whose abilities, even in their extemporary way, comes not short of the others, but their modesty and learning far exceeds the most of them.

But this matter is of so popular a nature, as some men knew it would not bear learned and sober debates, lest being convinced by the evidence of reason as well as laws, they should have been driven either to sin more against their knowledge, by taking away the Liturgy, or to displease some faction of the people by continuing the use of it.

Though I believe they have offended more considerable men, not only for their numbers and estates, but for their weighty and judicious piety, than those are whose weakness or giddiness they sought to gratify by taking it away.

One of the greatest faults some men found with the Common Prayer-book, I believe, was this, that it taught them to pray so oft for me; to which petitions they had not loyalty enough to say *Amen*, nor yet charity enough to forbear reproaches, and even cursings of me, in their own forms, instead of praying for me.

I wish their repentance may be their only punishment; that seeing the mischiefs which the disuse of public liturgies hath already produced, they may restore that credit, use, and reverence to them which by the ancient Churches were given to set forms of sound and wholesome words.

And Thou, O Lord, which art the same God, blessed for ever, whose mercies are full of variety, and yet of constancy, Thou deniest us not a new and fresh sense of our old and daily wants, nor despisest renewed affections joined to constant expressions.

Let us not want the benefit of Thy Church's united and well-advised devotions.

Let the matters of our prayers be agreeable to Thy will, which is always the same, and the fervency of our spirits to the motions of Thy Holy Spirit in us.

And then we doubt not but Thy spiritual perfections are such as Thou art neither to be pleased with affected novelties for matter or manner, nor offended with the pious constancy of our petitions in them both.

Whose variety or constancy Thou hast nowhere either forbidden or commanded, but left them to the piety and prudence of Thy Church, that both may be used, neither despised.

Keep men in that pious moderation of their judgments in matters of religion, that their ignorance may not offend others, nor their opinion of their own abilities tempt them to deprive others of what they may lawfully and devoutly use to help their infirmities.

And since the advantage of error consists in novelty and variety, as truth's in unity and constancy, suffer not Thy Church to be pestered with errors and deformed with undecencies in Thy service, under the pretence of variety and novelty, nor to be deprived of truth, unity, and order, under this fallacy, that constancy is the cause of formality.

Lord, keep us from formal hypocrisy in our own hearts, and then we know that praying to Thee, or praising of

Thee (with David and other holy men) in the same forms cannot hurt us.

Give us wisdom to amend what is amiss within us, and there will be less to mend without us.

Evermore defend and deliver Thy Church from the effects of blind zeal and overbold devotion.

XVII.

OF THE DIFFERENCES BETWEEN THE KING AND THE TWO HOUSES, IN POINT OF CHURCH GOVERNMENT.

TOUCHING the government of the Church by bishops, the common jealousy hath been that I am earnest and resolute to maintain it, not so much out of piety as policy and reason of State.

Wherein so far, indeed, reason of State doth induce me to approve that government above any other, as I find it impossible for a prince to preserve the State in quiet, unless he hath such an influence upon Churchmen, and they such a dependence on him, as may best restrain the seditious exorbitancies of ministers' tongues; who with the keys of heaven have so far the keys of the people's hearts, as they prevail much by their oratory to let in or shut out both peace and loyalty.

So that I being (as King) instructed by God and the laws with the good both of Church and State, I see no reason I should give up, or weaken by any change, that power and influence which in right and reason I ought to have over both.

The removing bishops out of the House of Peers (of which I have elsewhere given an account) was sufficient to take off any suspicion that I incline to them for any use to be made of their votes in State affairs; though, indeed, I never thought any bishop worthy to sit in that House who would not vote according to his conscience.

I must now in charity be thought desirous to preserve that government in its right constitution, as a matter of religion, wherein both my judgment if fully satisfied that it hath of all other the fullest Scripture grounds, and also the constant practice of all Christian Churches: till of late years the tumultuariness of people, or the factiousness and pride of presbyters, or the covetousness of some states and princes, gave occasion to some men's wits to invent new models, and propose them under the specious titles of "Christ's Government, Sceptre, and Kingdom," the better to serve their turns, to whom the change was beneficial.

They must give me leave, having none of their temptations to invite me to alter the government of bishops (that I may have a title to their estates) not to believe their pretended grounds to any new ways; contrary to the full and constant testimony of all history, sufficiently convincing unbiassed men, that as the primitive Churches were undoubtedly governed by the Apostles and their immediate successors, the first and best bishops, so it cannot in reason or charity be supposed that all Churches in the world should either be ignorant of the rule by them prescribed, or so soon deviate from their divine and holy pattern: that since the first age, for fifteen hundred years, not one example can be produced of any settled Church wherein were many ministers and congregations, which had not some bishop above them, under whose jurisdiction and government they were.

Whose constant and universal practice agreeing with so large and evident Scripture directions and examples as are set down in the Epistles to Timothy and Titus, for the settling of that government, not in the persons only of Timothy and Titus, but in the succession; the want of government being that which the Church can no more dispense with in point of well-being, than the want of the Word and Sacraments in point of being.

I wonder how men came to look with so envious an eye upon bishops' power and authority, as to oversee both the ecclesiastical use of them and Apostolical constitution; which to me seems no less evidently set forth, as to the main scope and design of those Epistles, for the settling of a peculiar office, power, and authority in them, as president bishops above others, in point of ordination, censures, and other acts of ecclesiastical discipline, than those shorter characters of the qualities and duties of presbyter bishops and deacons are described in some parts of the same Epistles; who in the latitude and community of the name were then, and may now, not improperly be called bishops, as to the oversight and care of single congregations committed to them by the Apostles, or those Apostolical bishops who, as Timothy and Titus, succeeded them in that ordinary power, there assigned over larger divisions in which were many presbyters.

The humility of those first bishops avoiding the eminent title of Apostles, as a name in the Church's style appropriated from its common notion (of 'a messenger,' or 'one sent') to that special dignity which had extraordinary call, mission, gifts, and power immediately from Christ, they contented themselves with the ordinary titles of Bishops and Presbyters; until use (the great arbitrator of words, and master of language) finding reason to distinguish by a peculiar name those persons whose power and office were indeed distinct from and above all other in the Church, as succeeding the Apostles in the ordinary and constant power of governing the Churches (the honour of whose name they moderately, yet commendably, declined), all Christian Churches, submitting to that special authority, appropriated also the name of Bishop, without any suspicion or reproach of arrogancy, to those who were by apostolical propagation rightly descended and invested into that highest and largest power of governing even the most pure and primitive Churches; which, without all doubt, had many such holy bishops, after the pattern of Timothy and Titus, whose special power is not more clearly set down in those Epistles (the chief grounds and limits of all episcopal claim as from divine right) than are the characters of these perilous times, and those men that make them such; who, not enduring sound doctrine and clear testimonies of all Churches' practice, are most perverse disputers and proud usurpers against true Episcopacy; who, if they be not traitors and boasters, yet they seem to be very covetous, heady, highminded, inordinate, and fierce, lovers of themselves, having much of the form, little of the power of godliness.

Who, by popular heaps of weak, light, and unlearned teachers, seek to overlay and smother the pregnancy and authority of that power of Episcopal government, which, beyond all equivocation and vulgar fallacy of names, is most convincingly set forth both by Scripture and all after-histories of the Church.

This I write rather like a divine than a prince, that posterity may see (if ever these papers be public) that I had fair grounds, both from Scripture canons and ecclesiastical examples, whereon my judgment was stated for Episcopal government.

Nor was it any policy of State, or obstinacy of will, or partiality of affection, either to the men or their function, which fixed me; who cannot in point of worldly respects be so considerable to me as to recompense the injuries and losses I and my dearest relations, with my kingdoms, have sustained and hazarded, chiefly at first upon this quarrel.

And not only in religion, of which Scripture is the best rule, and the Church's universal practice the best commentary, but also in right season and the true nature of government, it cannot be thought that an orderly subordination among presbyters or ministers should be any more against Christianity than it is in all secular and civil governments, where parity breeds confusion and faction.

I can no more believe that such order is inconsistent with true religion, than good features are with beauty, or numbers with harmony.

Nor is it likely that God, who appointed several orders and a prelacy in the government of His Church among the Jewish priests, should abhor or forbid them among Christian ministers, who have as much of the principles of schism and division as other men; for preventing and suppressing of which, the Apostolical wisdom (which was divine), after that Christians were multiplied to many congregations, and presbyters with them, appointed this way of government, which might best preserve order and union with authority.

So that I conceive it was not the favour of princes, or ambition of presbyters, but the wisdom and piety of the Apostles that first settled bishops in the Church; which authority they constantly used and enjoyed in those times which were purest for religion, though sharpest for persecution.

Not that I am against the managing of this presidency and authority in one man, by the joint counsel and consent of many presbyters: I have offered to restore that, as a fit means to avoid those errors, corruptions, and partialities which are incident to any one man; also to avoid tyranny, which becomes no Christians, least of all Churchmen; besides, it will be a means to take away that burthen and odium of affairs which may lie too heavy on one man's shoulders, as, indeed, I think it formerly did on the bishops here.

Nor can I see what can be more agreeable both to

reason and religion than such a frame of government which is paternal, not magisterial, and wherein not only the necessity of avoiding faction and confusion, emulations and contempts, which are prone to arise among equals in power and function, but also the differences of some ministers' gifts, and aptitudes for government above others, doth invite to employ them in reference to those abilities wherein they are eminent.

Nor is this judgment of mine touching Episcopacy any pre-occupation of opinion, which will not admit any oppositions against it. It is well known I have endeavoured to satisfy myself in what the chief patrons for other ways can say against this or for theirs; and I find, as they have far less of Scripture grounds and of reason, so for examples and practice of the Church, or testimonies of histories, they are wholly destitute, wherein the whole stream runs so for Episcopacy, that there is not the least rivulet for any others.

As for those obtruded examples of some late reformed Churches (for many retain bishops still) whom necessity of times and affairs rather excuseth than commendeth for their inconformity to all antiquity, I could never see any reason why Churches orderly reformed, and governed by bishops, should be forced to conform to those few rather than to the Catholic example of all ancient Churches which needed no reformation, and to those Churches at this day, who, governed by bishops in all the Christian world, are many more than Presbyterians or Independents can pretend to be; all whom the Churches in my three kingdoms lately governed by bishops would equalize, I think, if not exceed.

Nor is it any point of wisdom or charity, where Christians differ (as many do in some points) there to widen the differences, and at once to give all the Christian world (except a handful of some Protestants) so great a scandal in point of Church government; whom, though you may convince of their errors in some points of doctrine, yet you shall never persuade them that to complete their reformation they must necessarily desert and wholly cast off that government which they and all before them have ever owned as Catholic, Primitive, and Apostolical, so far that never schismatics nor heretics (except those Arians) have strayed from the unity and conformity of the Church in that point, ever having bishops above presbyters.

Besides, the late general approbation and submission to this government of bishops by the clergy as well as the laity of these kingdoms, is a great confirmation of my judgment, and their inconstancy is a great prejudice against their novelty. I cannot in charity so far doubt of their learning or integrity as if they understood not what heretofore they did, or that they did conform contrary to their consciences. So that their facility and levity is never to be excused, who, before ever the point of Church-government had any free and impartial debate, contrary to their former oaths and practice, against their obedience to the laws in force, and against my consent, have not only quite cried down the government by bishops, but have approved and encouraged the violent and most illegal stripping of all the bishops, and many other Churchmen, of all their due authority and revenues, even to the selling away and utter alienation of those Church-lands from any ecclesiastical uses. So great a power hath the stream of times and the prevalency of parties over some men's judgments, of whose so sudden and so total change little reason can be given, besides the Scots' army coming into England.

But the folly of these men will at last punish itself, and the deserters of Episcopacy will appear the greatest enemies to and betrayers of their own interest; for Presbytery is never so considerable or effectual as when it is joined to and crowned with Episcopacy. All ministers will find as great a difference, in point of thriving, between the favour of the people and of princes, as plants do between being watered by hand or by the sweet and liberal dews of heaven.

The tenuity and contempt of clergymen will soon let them see what a poor carcass they are when parted from the influence of that head to whose supremacy they have been sworn.

A little moderation might have prevented great mischiefs. I am firm to primitive Episcopacy, not to have it extirpated, if I can hinder it. Discretion without passion might easily reform whatever the rust of times, or indulgence of laws, or corruption of manners have brought upon it; it being a gross vulgar error to impute to or to revenge upon the function the faults of times or persons, which seditious and popular principle and practice all wise men abhor.

For those secular additaments and ornaments of authority, civil honour and estate, which my predecessors and Christian princes in all countries have annexed to bishops and Churchmen, I look upon them but as just rewards of their learning and piety, who are fit to be in any degree of Church government; also enablements to works of charity and hospitality, meet strengthenings of their authority in point of respect and observance, which in peaceful times is hardly paid to any governors by the measure of their virtues so much as by that of their estates, poverty and meanness exposing them and their authority to the contempt of licentious minds and manners, which persecuting times much restrained.

I would have such men bishops as are most worthy of those encouragements, and best able to use them. If at any time my judgment of men failed, my good intentions made my error venial; and some bishops I am sure I had whose learning, gravity, and piety no men of any worth or forehead can deny. But of all men, I would have Churchmen, especially the governors, to be redeemed from that vulgar neglect which (besides an innate principle of vicious opposition which is in all men against those that seem to reprove or restrain them) will necessarily follow both the Presbyterian party, which make all ministers equal, and the Independent inferiority, which sets their pastors below the people.

This for my judgment touching Episcopacy; wherein God knows, I do not gratify any design or passion with the least perverting of truth.

And now I appeal to God above and all the Christian world whether it be just for subjects or pious for Christians, by violence and infinite indignities, with servile restraints to seek to force me their King and Sovereign, as some men have endeavoured to do, against all these grounds of my judgment, to consent to their weak and divided novelties.

The greatest pretender of them desires not more than I do that the Church should be governed as Christ hath appointed, in true reason and in Scripture, of which I could never see any probable show for any other ways: who either content themselves with the examples of some Churches in their infancy and solitude, when one presbyter might serve one congregation in a city or country, or else they deny these most evident truths, that the Apostles were bishops over those presbyters they ordained, as well as over the Churches they planted; and that government being necessary for the Church's well-being, when multiplied and sociated, must also necessarily descend from the Apostles to others, after the example of that power and superiority they had above others, which could not end with their persons, since the use and ends of such government still continue.

It is most sure that the purest primitive and best Churches flourished under Episcopacy, and may so still, if ignorance, superstition, avarice, revenge, and other disorderly and disloyal passions had not so blown up some men's minds against it, that what they want of reasons or primitive patterns, they supply with violence and oppression; wherein some men's zeal for bishop's lands, houses, and revenues, hath set them on work to eat up Episcopacy; which, however other men esteem, to me is no less sin than sacrilege, or a robbery of God (the Giver of all we have) of that portion which devout minds have thankfully given again to Him, in giving it to His Church and Prophets; through whose hands He graciously accepts even a cup of cold water as a libation offered to Himself.

Furthermore, as to my particular engagement above other men by an oath agreeable to my judgment, I am solemnly obliged to preserve that government and the rights of the Church.

Were I convinced of the unlawfulness of the function, as Antichristian, (which some men boldly, but weakly, calumniate,) I could soon with judgment break that oath, which erroneously was taken by me.

But being daily, by the best disquisition of truth, more confirmed in the reason and religion of that to which I am sworn, how can any man that wisheth not my damnation persuade me at once to so notorious and combined sins of sacrilege and perjury? besides the many personal injustices I must do to many worthy men, who are as legally invested in their estates as any who seek to deprive them; and they have by no law been convicted of those crimes which might forfeit their estates and livelihoods.

I have oft wondered how men pretending to tenderness of conscience and reformation, can at once tell me that my Coronation Oath binds me to consent to whatsoever they shall propound to me (which they urge with such violence), though contrary to all that rational and religious freedom which every man ought to preserve, and of which they seem so tender in their own votes; yet at the same time these men will needs persuade me that I must and ought to dispense with, and roundly break that part of my oath which binds me (agreeable to the best light of reason and religion I have) to maintain the government and legal rights of the Church. It is strange my oath should be valid in that part which both myself and all men in their own case esteem injurious and unreasonable, as being against the very natural essential liberty of our souls; yet it should be invalid, and to be broken in another clause, wherein I think myself justly obliged both to God and man.

Yet upon this rack chiefly have I been held so long by some men's ambitious covetousness and sacrilegious cruelty, torturing (with me) both Church and State in civil dissensions, till I shall be forced to consent and declare that I do approve what, God knows, I utterly dislike, and in my soul abhor, as many ways highly against reason, justice, and religion; and whereto if I should shamefully and dishonourably give my consent, yet should I not by so doing satisfy the divided interests and opinions of those parties which contend with each other as well as both against me and Episcopacy.

Nor can my late condescending to the Scots in point of Church government be rightly objected against me as an inducement for me to consent to the like in my other kingdoms; for it should be considered that Episcopacy was not so rooted and settled there as it is here, nor I, in that respect, so strictly bound to continue it in that kingdom as in this; for what I think in my judgment best I may not think so absolutely necessary for all places and at all times.

If any shall impute my yielding to them as my failing and sin, I can easily acknowledge it; but that is no argument to do so again, or much worse, I being now more convinced in that point: nor, indeed, hath my yielding to them been so happy and successful as to encourage me to grant the like to others.

Did I see anything more of Christ as to meekness, justice, order, charity, and loyalty in those that pretend to other modes of government, I might suspect my judgment to be biassed or forestalled with some prejudice and wontedness of opinion; but I have hitherto so much cause to suspect the contrary in the manners of many of those men, that I cannot from them gain the least reputation for their new ways of government.

Nor can I find that in any reformed Churches (whose patterns are so cried up and obtruded upon the Churches under my dominion) either learning or religion, works of piety or charity, have so flourished beyond what they have done in my kingdoms, by God's blessing, which might make me believe either Presbytery or Independency have a more benign influence upon the Church and men's hearts and lives, than Episcopacy in its right constitution.

The abuses of which deserve to be extirpated as much as the use retained; for I think it far better to hold to primitive and uniform antiquity, than to comply with divided novelty.

A right Episcopacy would at once satisfy all just desires and interests of good bishops, humble presbyters, and sober people; so as Church affairs should be managed neither with tyranny, parity, nor popularity; neither bishops ejected, nor presbyters despised, nor people oppressed.

And in this integrity both of my judgment and conscience I hope God will preserve me.

For Thou, O Lord, knowest my uprightness and tenderness. As Thou hast set me to be a Defender of the Faith *and a protector of Thy Church, so suffer me not by any violence to be overborne against my conscience.*

Arise, O Lord, maintain Thine own cause; let not Thy Church be deformed as to that government, which, derived from Thy Apostles, hath been retained in purest and primitive times, till the revenues of the Church became the object of secular envy, which seeks to rob it of all the encouragements of learning and religion.

Make me, as a good Samaritan, compassionate and helpful to Thy afflicted Church, which some men have wounded and robbed, others pass by without regard, either to pity or relieve.

As my power is from Thee, so give me grace to use it for Thee.

And though I am not suffered to be master of my other rights as a King, yet preserve me in that liberty of reason, love of religion, and Thy Church's welfare, which are fixed in my conscience as a Christian.

Preserve from sacrilegious invasions those temporal blessings which Thy providence hath bestowed on Thy Church for Thy glory.

Forgive their sins and errors who have deserved Thy just permission thus to let in the wild boar and subtle foxes to waste and deform Thy vineyard which Thy right hand hath planted, and the dew of heaven so long watered to a happy and flourishing estate.

O let me not bear the infamous brand to all posterity of being the first Christian King in this kingdom who should consent to the oppression of Thy Church and the Fathers of it; whose errors I would rather, with Constantine, cover with silence, and reform with meekness, than expose their persons and sacred functions to vulgar contempt.

Thou, O Lord, seest how much I have suffered with and for Thy Church; make no long tarrying, O my God to deliver both me and it from unreasonable men, whose counsels have brought forth and continue such violent confusions, by a precipitant destroying the ancient boundaries of Thy Church's peace, thereby letting in all manner of errors, schisms, and disorders.

O Thou God of order and of truth, in Thy good time abate the malice, assuage the rage, and confound all the mischievous devices of Thine, mine, and Thy Church's enemies.

That I, and all that love Thy Church, may sing praises to Thee, and ever magnify Thy salvation, even before the sons of men.

XVIII.

Upon Uxbridge Treaty, and other Offers made by the King.

I LOOK upon the way of treaties as a retiring from fighting like beasts, to arguing like men, whose strength should be more in their understandings than in their limbs.

And though I could seldom get opportunities to treat, yet I never wanted either desire or disposition to it, having greater confidence of my reason than my sword. I was so wholly resolved to yield to the first, that I thought neither myself nor others should need to use the second, if once we rightly understood each other.

Nor did I ever think it a diminution of me to prevent them with expresses of my desires, and even importunities to treat; it being an office not only of humanity rather to use reason than force, but also of Christianity, to *seek peace and ensue it.*

As I was very unwillingly compelled to defend myself with arms, so I very willingly embraced anything tending to peace:

The events of all war by the sword being very dubious, and of a civil war uncomfortable, the end hardly recompensing, and late repairing the mischief of the means.

Nor did any success I had ever enhance with me the price of peace, as earnestly desired by me as any man, though I was like to pay dearer for it than any man. All that I sought to reserve was mine honour and my conscience; the one I could not part with as a King, the other as a Christian.

The Treaty at Uxbridge gave the fairest hopes of an happy composure; had others applied themselves to it with the same moderation as I did, I am confident the war had then ended.

I was willing to condescend as far as reason, honour, and conscience would give me leave; nor were the remaining differences so essential to my people's happiness, or of such consequence as in the least kind to have hindered my subjects' either security or prosperity, for they better enjoyed both many years before ever those demands were made; some of which to deny I think the greatest justice to myself and favour to my subjects.

I see jealousies are not so easily allayed as they are raised. Some men are more afraid to retreat from violent engagements, than to engage; what is wanting in equity, must be made up in pertinacy. Such as had little to enjoy in peace, or to lose in war, studied to render the very name of *peace* odious and suspected.

In Church affairs, where I had least liberty of prudence, having so many strict ties of conscience upon me, yet I was willing to condescend so far to the settling of them as might have given fair satisfaction to all men whom faction, covetousness, or superstition had not engaged more than any true zeal, charity, or love of reformation.

I was content to yield to all that might seem to advance true piety. I only sought to continue what was necessary in point of order, maintenance, and authority, to the Church's government, and what I am persuaded (as I have elsewhere set down my thoughts more fully) is most agreeable to the true principles of all government, raised to its full stature and perfection, as also to the primitive Apostolical pattern, and the practice of the Universal Church conform thereto.

From which wholly to recede, without any probable reason urged or answered, only to satisfy some men's wills and phantasies (which yet agree not among themselves in any point, but that of extirpating Episcopacy, and fighting against me,) must needs argue such a softness and infirmity of mind in me as will rather part with God's truth than man's peace, and rather lose the Church's honour, than cross some men's factious humours.

God knows, and time will discover, who were most to blame for the unsuccessfulness of that Treaty, and who must bear the guilt of after-calamities. I believe I am very excusable both before God and all unpassionate men who have seriously weighed those transactions, wherein I endeavoured no less the restoration of peace to my people, than the preservation of my own crowns to my posterity.

Some men have that height, as to interpret all fair condescendings as arguments of feebleness, and glory most in an unflexible stiffness when they see others most supple and inclinable to them.

A grand maxim with them was always to ask something which in reason and honour must be denied, that they might have some colour to refuse all that was in other things granted; setting peace at as high a rate as the worst effects of war; endeavouring first to make me destroy myself by dishonourable concessions, that so they might have the less to do.

This was all which that treaty or any other produced, to let the world see how little I would deny, or they grant, in order to the public peace.

That it gave occasion to some men's further restiveness is imputable to their own depraved tempers, not to any concessions or negations of mine: I have always the content of what I offered and they the regret and blame for what they refused.

The highest tide of success set me not above a treaty, nor the lowest ebb below a fight; though I never thought it any sign of true valour to be prodigal of men's lives, rather than to be drawn to produce our own reasons, or subscribe to other men's.

That which made me for the most part presage the unsuccessfulness of any treaty, was some men's unwillingness to treat; which implied some things were to be gained by the sword, whose unreasonableness they were loth to have fairly scanned, being more proper to be acted by soldiers than counsellors.

I pray God forgive them that were guilty of that Treaty's breaking, and give them grace to make their advantages gotten by the sword a better opportunity to use such moderation as was then wanting; that so, though peace were for our sins justly deferred, yet at last it may be happily obtained; what we could not get by our treaties, we may gain by our prayers.

O Thou that art the God of reason and of peace, who disdainest not to treat with sinners, preventing them with offers of atonement, and beseeching them to be reconciled with Thyself, who wantest not power or justice to destroy them, yet aboundest in mercy to save; soften our hearts by the blood of our Redeemer, and persuade us to accept of peace with Thyself, and both to procure and preserve peace among ourselves, as men and Christians. How oft have I entreated for peace, but when I speak thereof, they make them ready to war.

Condemn us not to our Passions, which are destructive both of ourselves and of others.

Clear up our understandings to see Thy truth, both in reason, as men, and in religion, as Christians; and incline all our hearts to hold the unity of the spirit in the bond of peace.

Take from us that enmity which is now in our hearts against Thee, and give us that charity which should be among ourselves.

Remove the evils of war we have deserved, and bestow upon us that peace which only Christ our great Peacemaker can merit.

XIX.

Upon the Various Events of the War;
Victories and Defeats.

The various successes of this unhappy war have afforded me variety of good meditations. Sometimes God was pleased to try me with victory by worsting my enemies, that I might know how with moderation and thanks to own and use His power, who is only the true Lord of Hosts, able when He pleases to repress the confidence of those that fought against me with so great advantages for power and number.

From small beginnings on my part He let me see that I was not wholly forsaken by my people's love or His protection.

Other times God was pleased to exercise my patience, and teach me not to trust in the arm of flesh, but in the living God.

My sins sometimes prevailed against the justice of my cause, and those that were with me wanted not matter and occasion for His just chastisement both of them and me. Nor were my enemies less punished by that prosperity, which hardened them to continue that injustice by open hostility, which was begun by most riotous and unparliamentary tumults.

Their is no doubt but personal and private sins may oftimes overbalance the justice of public engagements; nor doth God account every gallant man (in the world's esteem) a fit instrument to assert in the way of war a righteous cause. The more men are prone to arrogate to their own skill, valour, and strength, the less doth God ordinarily work by them for His own glory.

I am sure the event or success can never state the justice of any cause, nor the peace of men's consciences, nor the eternal fate of their souls.

Those with me had, I think, clearly and undoubtedly for their justification the Word of God and the laws of the land together with their own oaths; all requiring obedience to my just commands, but to none other under heaven without me, or against me in the point of raising arms.

Those on the other side are forced to fly to the shifts of some pretended fears and wild fundamentals of State, as they call them, which actually overthrow the present fabric both of Church and State; being such imaginary reasons for self-defence as are most impertinent for those men to allege, who being my subjects were manifestly the first assaulters of me and the laws, first by unsuppressed tumults, after by listed forces. The same allegations they use will fit any faction that hath but power and confidence enough to second with the sword all their demands against the present laws and governors; which can never be such as some side or other will not find fault with, so as to urge what they call a reformation of them to a rebellion against them.

Some parasitic preachers have dared to call those martyrs who died fighting against me, the laws, their oaths, and the religion established; but sober Christians know that glorious title can with truth be applied only to those who sincerely preferred God's truth and their duty in all these particulars, before their lives, and all that was dear to them in this world; who having no advantageous designs by any innovation, were religiously sensible of those ties of God, the Church, and myself, which lay upon their souls, both for obedience and just assistance.

God could, and I doubt not but He did, through His mercy, crown many of them with eternal life whose lives were lost in so just a cause, the destruction of their bodies being sanctified as a means to save their souls.

Their wounds and temporal ruin serving as a gracious opportunity for their eternal health and happiness, while the evident approach of death did, through God's grace, effectually dispose their hearts to such humility, faith, and repentance, which, together with the rectitude of their present engagement, would fully prepare them for a better life than that which their enemies' brutish and disloyal fierceness could deprive them of, or, without repentance, hope to enjoy.

They have often indeed had the better against my side in the field, but never, I believe, at the bar of God's tribunal, or their own consciences; where they are more afraid to encounter those many pregnant reasons, both from law, allegiance, and all true Christian grounds, which conflict with and accuse them in their own thoughts, than they oft were in a desperate bravery to fight against those forces, which sometimes God gave me.

Whose condition, conquered and dying, I make no question but is infinitely more to be chosen by a sober man (that duly values his duty, his soul, and eternity, beyond the enjoyments of this present life,) than the most triumphant glory wherein their and mine enemies supervive; who can hardly avoid to be daily tormented by that horrid guilt wherewith their suspicious or now-convicted consciences do pursue them; especially since they and all the world have seen how false and unintended those pretensions were which they first set forth as the only plausible, though not justifiable, grounds of raising a war, and continuing it thus long against me, and the laws established, in whose safety and preservation all honest men think the welfare of their country doth consist.

For and with all which it is far more honourable and comfortable to suffer, than to prosper in their ruin and subversion.

I have often prayed that all on my side might join true piety with the sense of their loyalty, and be as faithful to God and their own souls as they were to me; that the defects of the one might not blast the endeavours of the other.

Yet I cannot think that any shows or truth of piety on the other side were sufficient to dispense with or expiate the defects of their duty and loyalty to me, which have so pregnant convictions on men's consciences, that even profaner men are moved by the sense of them to venture their lives for me.

I never had any victory which was without my sorrow,

because it was on mine own subjects, who, like Absalom, died many of them in their sin: and yet I never suffered any defeat which made me despair of God's mercy and defence.

I never desired such victories as might serve to conquer, but only restore the laws and liberties of my people; which I saw were extremely oppressed, together with my rights, by those men who were impatient of any just restraint.

When Providence gave me or denied me victory, my desire was neither to boast of my power, nor to charge God foolishly, who I believed at last would make all things to work together for my good.

I wished no greater advantages by the war than to bring my enemies to moderation, and my friends to peace.

I was afraid of the temptation of an absolute conquest, and never prayed more for victory over others than over myself. When the first was denied, the second was granted me, which God saw best for me.

The different events were but the methods of divine justice, by contrary winds, to winnow us; that by punishing our sins He might purge them from us, and by deferring peace He might prepare us more to prize and better to use so great a blessing.

My often messages for peace shewed that I delighted not in war: as my former concessions sufficiently testified how willingly I would have prevented it; and my total unpreparedness for it, how little I intended it.

The conscience of my innocency forbad me to fear a

war; but the love of my kingdoms commanded me, if possible, to avoid it.

I am guilty in this war of nothing but this, that I gave such advantages to some men by confirming their power, which they knew not to use with that modesty and gratitude which became their loyalty and my confidence.

Had I yielded less, I had been opposed less; had I denied more, I had been more obeyed.

It is now too late to review the occasions of the war; I wish only a happy conclusion of so unhappy beginnings. The inevitable fate of our sins was, no doubt, such as would no longer suffer the Divine Justice to be quiet: we having conquered His patience, are condemned by mutual conquerings to destroy one another; for the most prosperous successes on either side impair the welfare of the whole.

Those victories are still miserable that leave our sins unsubdued, flushing our pride, and animating to continue injuries.

Peace itself is not desirable, till repentance have prepared us for it.

When we fight more against ourselves and less against God, we shall cease fighting one against another. I pray God these may all meet in our hearts, and so dispose us to an happy conclusion of these civil wars, that I may know better to obey God and govern my people, and they may learn better to obey both God and me.

Nor do I desire any man should be further subject to me, than all of us may be subject to God.

O my God, make me content to be overcome, when Thou wilt have it so.

Teach me the noblest victory over myself and my enemies by patience, which was Christ's conquest, and may well become a Christian King.

Between both Thy hands, the right sometimes supporting and the left afflicting, fashion us to that frame of piety Thou likest best.

Forgive the pride that attends our prosperous, and the repinings which follow our disastrous events; when going forth in our own strength, Thou withdrawest Thine, and goest not forth with our armies.

Be Thou all, when we are something, and when we are nothing; that Thou mayest have the glory when we are in a victorious or inglorious condition.

Thou, O Lord, knowest how hard it is for me to suffer so much evil from my subjects, to whom I intend nothing but good; and I cannot but suffer in those evils which they compel me to inflict upon them, punishing myself in their punishments.

Since, therefore, both in conquering and being conquered I am still a sufferer, I beseech Thee to give me a double portion of Thy Spirit, and that measure of grace which only can be sufficient for me.

As I am most afflicted, so make me most reformed, that I may be not only happy to see an end of these civil distractions, but a chief instrument to restore and establish a firm and blessed peace to my kingdoms.

Stir up in all parties pious ambitions to overcome each other with reason, moderation, and such self-denial as becomes those who consider that our mutual divisions are our common distractions, and the union of all is every good man's chiefest interest.

If, O Lord, as for the sins of our peace Thou hast brought upon us the miseries of war, so for the sins of war Thou shouldst see fit still to deny us the blessing of peace, and so keep us in a circulation of miseries; yet give me, Thy servant, and all loyal (though afflicted) subjects, to enjoy that peace which the world can neither give to us nor take from us.

Impute not to me the blood of my subjects, which with infinite unwillingness and grief hath been shed by me in my just and necessary defence; but wash me with that precious blood which hath been shed for me by my great Peacemaker, Jesus Christ, who will, I trust, redeem me shortly out of all my troubles; for I know the triumphing of the wicked is but short and the joy of hypocrites is but for a moment.

XX.

Upon the Reformation of the Times.

No glory is more to be envied than that of due reforming either Church or State, when deformities are such that the perturbation and novelty are not like to exceed the benefit of reforming.

Although God should not honour me so far as to make me an instrument of so good a work, yet I should be glad to see it done.

As I was well pleased with this Parliament's first intentions to reform what the indulgence of times and corruption of manners might have depraved, so I am sorry to see, after the freedom of Parliament was by factious tumults oppressed, how little regard was had to the good laws established and the religion settled, which ought to be the first rule and standard of reforming; with how much partiality and popular compliance the passions and opinions of men have been gratified, to the detriment of the public, and the infinite scandal of the reformed religion.

What dissolutions of all order and government in the Church, what novelties of schisms and corrupt opinions, what indecencies and confusions in sacred administrations, what sacrilegious invasions upon the rights and revenues of the Church, what contempt and oppressions of the clergy, what injurious diminutions and persecutions of me have followed (as showers do warm gleams) the talk of reformation, all sober men are witnesses, and, with myself, sad spectators hitherto.

The great miscarriage, I think, is, that popular clamours and fury have been allowed the reputation of zeal and the public sense, so that the study to please some parties hath indeed injured all.

Freedom, moderation, and impartiality are sure the best tempers of reforming counsels and endeavours: what is acted by factions cannot but offend more than it pleaseth.

I have offered to put all differences in Church affairs and religion to the free consultation of a synod or convocation rightly chosen, the results of whose counsels, as they would have included the votes of all, so it's like they would have given most satisfaction to all.

The Assembly of Divines, whom the two Houses have applied, in an unwonted way, to advise of Church affairs, I dislike not further, than that they are not legally convened and chosen, nor act in the name of all the clergy of England, nor with freedom and impartiality can do anything, being limited and confined, if not over-awed, to do and declare what they do.

For I cannot think so many men, cried up for learning and piety, who formerly allowed the Liturgy and government of the Church of England as to the main, would have so suddenly agreed quite to abolish both of them (the last of which they knew to be of Apostolical institution at least, as of primitive and universal practice,) if they had been left to the liberty of their own suffrages; and if the influence of contrary factions had not by secret encroachments of hopes and fears prevailed upon them to comply with so great and dangerous innovations in the Church, without any regard to their own former judgment and practice, or to the common interest and honour of all the clergy, and in them for order, learning, and religion; against examples of all ancient Churches, the laws in force, and my consent, which is never to be gained against so pregnant light as in that point shines on my understanding.

For I conceive that where the Scripture is not so clear and punctual in precepts, there the constant and universal practice of the Church, in things not contrary to reason, faith, good manners, or any positive command, is the best rule that Christians can follow.

I was willing to grant or restore to Presbytery what with reason or discretion it can pretend to, in a conjuncture with Episcopacy; but for that wholly to invade the power, and by the sword to arrogate and quite abrogate the authority of that ancient order, I think neither just as to Episcopacy, nor safe for Presbytery, nor yet any way convenient for this Church or State.

A due reformation had easily followed moderate counsels, and such, I believe, as would have given more content even to the most of those divines who have been led on with much gravity and formality to carry on other men's designs, which no doubt many of them by this time discover, though they dare not but smother their frustrations and discontents.

The specious and popular titles of Christ's government, throne, sceptre, and kingdom (which certainly is not divided, nor hath two faces, as their parties now have at least,) as also the noise of a thorough reformation, may as easily be fixed on new models, as fair colours may be put to ill favoured figures.

The breaking of church windows, which time had sufficiently defaced; pulling down of crosses, which were but civil, not religious marks; defacing of the monuments and inscriptions of the dead, which served but to put posterity in mind to thank God for that clearer light wherein they live; the leaving of all ministers to their liberties and private abilities in the service of God, where no Christian can tell to what he may say *Amen*, nor what adventure he may make of seeming, at least, to consent to the errors, blasphemies, and ridiculous undecencies, which bold and ignorant men list to vent in their prayers, preaching, and other offices; the setting forth also of old catechisms and confessions of faith new drest, importing as much as if there had been no sound or clear doctrine of faith in this Church, before some four or five years' consultation had matured their thoughts, touching their first principles of religion :

All these and the like are the effects of popular, specious, and deceitful reformations, that they might not seem to have nothing to do, and may give some short flashes of content to the vulgar (who are taken with novelties, as children with babies, very much, but not very long): but all this amounts not to, nor can in justice merit the glory, of the Church's thorough reformation, since they leave all things more deformed, disorderly, and discontented, than when they begin, in point of piety, morality, charity, and good order.

Nor can they easily recompense or remedy the inconveniences and mischiefs which they have purchased so dearly, and which have and ever will necessarily ensue, till due remedies be applied.

I wish they would at last make it their unanimous work to do God's work, and not their own. Had religion been first considered, as it merited, much trouble might have been prevented.

But some men thought that the government of this

Church and State, fixed by so many laws and long customs, would not run into new moulds till they had first melted it in the fire of a civil war; by the advantages of which they resolved, if they prevailed, to make myself and all my subjects, fall down and worship the images they should form and set up. If there had been as much of Christ's spirit for meekness, wisdom, and charity in men's hearts as there was of His Name used in the pretensions to reform all to Christ's rule, it would certainly have obtained more of God's blessing, and produced more of Christ's glory, the Church's good, the honour of religion, and the Unity of Christians.

Public reformers had need first act in private, and practice that on their own hearts which they purpose to try on others; for deformities within will soon betray the pretenders of public reformation to such private designs as must needs hinder the public good.

I am sure the right methods of reforming the Church cannot consist with that of perturbing the civil state, nor can religion be justly advanced by depressing loyalty, which is one of the chiefest ingredients and ornaments of true religion, for next to *fear God* is *honour the King*.

I doubt not but Christ's kingdom may be set up without pulling down mine; nor will any men in impartial times appear good Christians that approve not themselves good subjects.

Christ's government will confirm mine, not overthrow it; since as I own mine from Him, so I desire to rule for His glory and His Church's good.

Had some men truly intended Christ's Government, or knew what it meant in ther hearts, they could never have been so ill governed in their words and actions both against me and one another.

As good ends cannot justify evil means, so nor will evil beginnings ever bring forth good conclusions, unless God, by a miracle of mercy, create light out of darkness, order out of our confusions, and peace out of our passions.

Thou, O Lord, who only canst give us beauty for ashes, and truth for hypocrisy, suffer us not to be miserably deluded with Pharisaical washings, instead of Christian reformings.

Our greatest deformities are within: make us the severest censurers and first reformers of our own souls.

That we may in clearness of judgment and uprightness of heart be a means to reform what is indeed amiss in Church and State.

Create in us clean hearts, O Lord, and renew right spirits within us; that we may do all by Thy directions, to Thy glory, and with Thy blessing.

Pity the deformities which some rash and cruel reformers have brought upon this Church and State; quench the fires which factions have kindled under the pretence of reforming.

As thou hast shewed the world, by their divisions and confusions, what is the pravity of some men's intentions, and weakness of their judgments, so bring us at last more refined out of these fires by the methods of Christian and charitable reformations, wherein nothing of ambition, revenge, covetousness, or sacrilege may have any influence upon their counsels whom Thy *providence in just and lawful ways shall intrust with so great, good, and now necessary a work. That I and my people may be so blest with inward piety, as may best teach us how to use the blessing of outward peace.*

XXI.

Upon His Majesty's Letters taken and divulged.

The taking of my letters was an opportunity which as the malice of mine enemies could hardly have expected, so that they knew not how with honour and civility to use it. Nor do I think, with sober and worthy minds, anything in them could tend to my reproach, as the odious divulging of them did to the infamy of the divulgers: the greatest experiments of virtue and nobleness being discovered in the greatest advantages against an enemy, and the greatest obligations being those which are put upon by them from whom we could least have expected them.

And such I should have esteemed the concealing of my papers, the freedom and secrecy of which commands a civility from all men not wholly barbarous, nor is there anything more inhuman than to expose them to public view.

Yet since Providence will have it so, I am content so much of my heart (which I study to approve to God's omniscience) should be discovered to the world, without any of those dresses or popular captations which some men use in their speeches and expresses. I wish my subjects had yet a clearer sight into my most retired thoughts, where they might discover how they are divided between the love and care I have, not more to preserve my own rights, than to procure their peace and happiness, and that extreme grief to see them both deceived and destroyed.

Nor can any men's malice be gratified further by my letters, than to see my constancy to my wife, the laws, and religion. Bees will gather honey where the spider sucks poison.

That I endeavour to avoid the pressure of my enemies by all fair and just correspondencies, no man can blame who loves me or the commonwealth, since my subjects can hardly be happy if I be miserable, or enjoy their peace and liberties while I am oppressed.

The world may see how some men's design, like Absalom's, is by enormous actions to widen differences, and exasperate all sides to such distances as may make all reconciliation desperate.

Yet, I thank God, I can not only with patience bear this as other indignities, but with charity forgive them.

The integrity of my intentions is not jealous of any injury my expressions can do them; for although the confidence of privacy may admit greater freedom in writing such letters, which may be liable to envious exceptions, yet the innocency of my chief purposes cannot be so stained or misinterpreted by them, as not to let all men see that I wish nothing more than an happy composure of differences with justice and honour, not more to my own than my people's content, who have any sparks of love or loyalty left in them; who by those my letters may be convinced that I can both mind and act my own and my kingdoms' affairs, so as becomes a prince; which mine enemies have always been very loth should be believed of me, as if I were wholly confined to the dictates and directions of others, whom they please to brand with the name of evil counsellors.

It is probable some men will now look upon me as my own counsellor, and having none else to quarrel with under that notion, they will hereafter confine their anger to myself: although I know they are very unwilling I should enjoy the liberty of my own thoughts, or follow the light of my own conscience, which they labour to bring into an absolute captivity to themselves; not allowing me to think their counsels to be other than good to me, which have so long maintained a war against me.

The victory they obtained that day, when my letters became their prize, had been enough to have satiated the most ambitious thirst of popular glory among the vulgar, with whom prosperity gains the greatest esteem and applause, as adversity exposeth to their greatest slighting and disrespect: as if good fortune were always the shadow of virtue and justice, and did not oftener attend vicious and injurious actions as to this world.

But I see no secular advantages seem sufficient to that cause which began with tumults, and depends chiefly upon the reputation with the vulgar.

They think no victories so effectual to their designs, as those that most rout and waste my credit with my people; in whose hearts they seek by all means to smother and extinguish all sparks of love, respect and loyalty to me, that they may never kindle again, so as to recover mine, the laws and the kingdoms' liberties, which some men seek to overthrow. The taking away of my credit is but a necessary preparation to the taking away of my life and my kingdoms: first, I must seem neither fit to live, nor worthy to reign; by exquisite methods of cunning and cruelty I must be compelled first to follow the funerals of my honour, and then be destroyed. But I know God's unerring and impartial justice can and will overrule the most perverse wills and designs of men; He is able, and, I hope, will turn even the worst of mine enemies' thoughts and actions to my good.

Nor do I think that by the surprise of my letters I have lost any more than so many papers: how much they have lost of that reputation for civility and humanity, (which ought to be paid to all men, and most becomes such as pretend to religion,) besides that of respect and honour which they owe to their king, present and aftertimes will judge. And I cannot think that their own consciences are so stupid, as not to inflict upon them some secret impressions of that shame and dishonour which attends all unworthy actions, have they never so much of public flattery and popular countenance.

I am sure they can never expect the divine approbation of such indecent actions, if they do but remember how God blest the modest respect and filial tenderness which Noah's sons bare to their father; nor did his open infirmity justify Cham's impudency, or exempt him from the curse of being servant of servants: which curse much needs be on them who seek by dishonourable actions to please the vulgar, and confirm by ignoble acts their dependence upon the people.

Nor can their malicious intentions be ever either excusable or prosperous, who thought by this means to expose me to the highest reproach and contempt of my people: forgetting that duty of modest concealment which they owed to the father of their country, in case they had discovered any real uncomeliness, which, I thank God, they did not; who can, and, I believe, hath made me more respected in the hearts of many, (as He did David,) to whom they thought, by publishing my private letters, to have rendered me as *a vile person*, not fit to be trusted, or considered under any notion of majesty.

But Thou, O Lord, whose wise and all-disposing providence ordereth the greatest contingencies of human affairs, make me to see the constancy of Thy mercies to me in the greatest advantages Thou seemest to give the malice of my enemies against me.

As Thou didst blast the counsel of Ahithophel, turning it to David's good and his own ruin, so canst Thou defeat their design who intended, by publishing my private letters, nothing else but to render me more odious and contemptible to my people.

I must first appeal to Thy omniscience, who canst witness with my integrity how unjust and false those scandalous misconstructions are which my enemies endeavour by those papers of mine to represent to the world.

Make the evil they imagined, and displeasure they intended thereby against me, so to return on their own heads, that they may be ashamed, and covered with their own confusion as with a cloak.

Thou seest how mine enemies use all means to cloud mine honour, to pervert my purposes, and to slander the footsteps of Thine anointed.

But give me an heart content to be dishonoured for Thy sake and Thy Church's good.

Fix in me a purpose to honour Thee, and then I know Thou wilt honour me, either by restoring to me the enjoyment of that power and majesty which Thou hast suffered some men to seek to deprive me of; or by bestowing on me that crown of Christian patience which knows how to serve Thee in honour or dishonour, in good report or evil.

Thou, O Lord, art the fountain of goodness and honour, Thou art clothed with excellent majesty; make me to partake of Thy excellency for wisdom, justice, and mercy, and I shall not want that degree of honour and majesty which becomes the place in which Thou hast set me, who art the lifter up of my head, and my salvation.

Lord, by Thy grace lead me to Thy glory, which is both true and eternal.

XXII.

Upon His Majesty's leaving Oxford, and going to the Scots.

Although God hath given me three kingdoms, yet in these He hath not left me any place where I may with safety and honour rest my head; shewing me that Himself is the safest refuge, and the strongest tower of defence, in which I may put my trust.

In these extremities I look not to man so much as to God: He will have it thus; that I may wholly cast myself and my now distressed affairs upon His mercy, who hath both the hearts and hands of all men in His dispose.

What Providence denies to force, it may grant to prudence: necessity is now my counsellor, and commands me to study my safety by a disguised withdrawing from my chiefest strength, and adventuring upon their loyalty who first began my troubles. Haply God may make them a means honourably to compose them.

This my confidence of them may disarm and overcome them: my rendering my person to them may engage their affections to me, who have oft professed, "They fought not against me, but for me."

I must now resolve the riddle of their loyalty, and give them opportunity to let the world see they mean not what they do, but what they say.

Yet must God be my chiefest guard, and my conscience both my counsellor and my comforter. Though I put my body into their hands, yet I shall reserve my soul to God and myself; nor shall any necessities compel me to desert mine honour, or swerve from my judgment.

What they sought to take by force, shall now be given them in such a way of unusual confidence of them, as may make them ashamed not to be really such as they ought, and professed to be.

God sees it not enough to deprive me of all military power to defend myself; but to put me upon using their power, who seem to fight against me, yet ought in duty to defend me.

So various are all human affairs, and so necessitous may the state of princes be, that their greatest danger may be in their supposed safety, and their safety in their supposed danger.

I must now leave those that have adhered to me, and apply to those that have opposed me: this method of peace may be more prosperous than that of war, both to stop the effusion of blood, and to close those wounds already made. And in it I am no less solicitous for my friends' safety than mine own: choosing to venture myself upon further hazards, rather than expose their resolute loyalty to all extremities.

It is some skill in play to know when a game is lost: better fairly to give over than to contest in vain.

I must now study to reinforce my judgment and fortify my mind with reason and religion; that I may not seem to offer up my soul's liberty, or make my conscience their captive, who ought at first to have used arguments, not arms, to have persuaded my consent to their new demands.

I thank God, no success darkens or disguises truth to me; and I shall no less conform my words to my inward dictates now, than if they had been, as the words of a king ought to be, among loyal subjects, *full of power.*

Reason is the divinest power; I shall never think myself weakened, while I may make full and free use of that. No eclipse of outward fortune shall rob me of that light: what God hath denied of outward strength, His grace, I hope, will supply with inward resolutions; not morosely to deny what is fit to be granted, but not to grant anything which reason and religion bids me deny.

I shall never think myself less than myself, while I am able thus to preserve the integrity of my conscience, the only jewel now left me which is worth keeping.

O Thou Sovereign of our souls, the only Commander of our consciences, though I know not what to do, yet mine eyes are toward Thee; to the protection of Thy mercy I still commend myself.

As Thou hast preserved me in the day of battle, so Thou canst still shew me Thy strength in my weakness.

Be Thou unto me in my darkest night a pillar of fire, to enlighten and direct me; in the day of my hottest affliction be also a pillar of cloud to overshadow and protect me; be to me both a sun and a shield.

Thou knowest that it is not any perverseness of will, but just persuasions of honour, reason, and religion which have made me thus far to hazard my person, peace, and safety, against those that by force have sought to wrest them from me.

Suffer not my just resolutions to abate with my outward forces; let a good conscience always accompany me in my greatest solitude and desertions.

Suffer me not to betray the powers of reason and that fortress of my soul which I am entrusted to keep for Thee.

Lead me in the paths of Thy righteousness, and shew me Thy Salvation.

Make my ways to please Thee, and then Thou wilt make mine enemies to be at peace with me.

XXIII.

Upon the Scots delivering the King to the English, and his Captivity at Holdenby.

Yet may I justify those Scots to all the world in this, that they have not deceived me, for I never trusted to them further than to men: if I am sold by them I am only sorry that they should do it; and that my price should be so much above my Saviour's.

These are but further essays which God will have me make of man's uncertainty, the more to fix me on Himself, who never faileth them that trust in Him. Though the reeds of Egypt break under the hand of him that leans on them; yet the rock of Israel will be an everlasting stay and defence.

God's providence commands me to retire from all to Himself, that in Him I may enjoy myself, whom I lose while I let out my hopes to others.

The solitude and captivity to which I am now reduced, gives me leisure enough to study the world's vanity and inconstancy.

God sees it fit to deprive me of wife, children, army, friends, and freedom, that I may be wholly His who alone is all.

I care not much to be reckoned among the unfortunate, if I be not in the black list of irreligious and sacrilegious princes.

No restraint shall ensnare my soul in sin, nor gain that of me which may make my enemies more insolent, my friends ashamed, or my name accursed.

They have no great cause to triumph that they have got my person into their power, since my soul is still my own: nor shall they ever gain my consent against my conscience.

What they call obstinacy, I know God accounts honest constancy, from which reason and religion, as well as honour, forbid me to recede.

'Tis evident now, that it was not evil counsellors with me, but a good conscience in me, which hath been fought against; nor did they ever intend to bring me to my parliament, till they had brought my mind to their obedience.

Should I grant what some men desire, I should be such as they wish me; not more a king, and far less both man and Christian.

What tumults and armies could not obtain, neither shall restraint; which though it have as little of safety to a prince, yet it hath not more of danger.

The fear of men shall never be my snare, nor shall the love of any liberty entangle my soul: better others betray me than myself, and that the price of my liberty should be my conscience. The greatest injuries my enemies seek to inflict upon me cannot be without my own consent.

While I can deny with reason, I shall defeat the greatest impressions of their malice, who neither know how to use worthily what I have already granted, nor what to require more of me but this, that I would seem willing to help them to destroy myself and mine.

Although they should destroy me, yet they shall have no cause to despise me.

Neither liberty nor life are so dear to me as the peace of my conscience, the honour of my crowns, and the welfare of my people; which my word may injure more than any war can do, while I gratify a few to oppress all.

The laws will by God's blessing revive, with the love and loyalty of my subjects, if I bury them not by my consent, and cover them in that grave of dishonour and injustice which some men's violence hath digged for them.

If my captivity or death must be the price of their redemption, I grudge not to pay it.

No condition can make a king miserable, which carries not with it his soul's, his people's, and prosperity's thraldom.

After times may see what the blindness of this age will not; and God may at length shew my subjects, that I choose rather to suffer for them than with them. Haply I might redeem myself to some show of liberty, if I would consent to enslave them. I had rather hazard the ruin of one king, than to confirm many tyrants over them; from whom I pray God deliver them, whatever becomes of me, whose solitude has not left me alone.

For Thou, O God, infinitely good and great, art with me, whose presence is better than life, and whose service is perfect freedom.

Own me for Thy servant, and I shall never have cause to complain for want of that liberty which becomes a man, a Christian, and a King.

Bless me still with reason as a man, with religion as a Christian, and with constancy in justice as a King.

Though Thou suffered me to be stript of all outward ornaments, yet preserve me ever in those enjoyments wherein I may enjoy Thyself, and which cannot be taken from me against my will.

Let no fire of affliction boil over my passion to any impatience or sordid fears.

There be many say of me, there is no help for me: do Thou lift up the light of Thy countenance upon me, and I shall never want safety, liberty, nor majesty.

Give me that measure of patience and constancy which my condition now requires.

My strength is scattered, my expectation from men

defeated, my person restrained: O be not Thou far from me, lest my enemies prevail too much against me.

I am become a wonder and a scorn to many: O be Thou my helper and defender.

Shew some token upon me for good, that they that hate me may be ashamed, because Thou, Lord, hast holpen and comforted me. Establish me with Thy free spirit, that I may do and suffer Thy will as Thou wouldst have me.

Be merciful to me, O Lord, for my soul trusteth in Thee; yea, and in the shadow of Thy wings will I make my refuge, until these calamities be overpast.

Arise to deliver me, make no long tarrying, O my God. Though Thou killest me, yet will I trust in Thy mercy and my Saviour's merit.

I know that my Redeemer liveth: though Thou leadest me through the vale and shadow of death, yet shall I fear none ill.

XXIV.

Upon their denying His Majesty the Attendance of his Chaplains, viz., Dr. Juxon, Bishop of London; Dr. Duppa, Bishop of Salisbury; Dr. Sheldon, Dr. Hammond, Dr. Holdsworth, Dr. Sanderson, Dr. Turner, Dr. Heywood.

When Providence was pleased to deprive me of all other civil comforts and secular attendants, I thought the absence of them all might best be supplied by the attendance of some of my chaplains; whom for their function I reverence, and for their fidelity I have cause to love. By their learning, piety, and prayers, I hoped to be either better enabled to sustain the want of all other enjoyments, or better fitted for the recovery and use of them in God's good time: so reaping by their pious help a spiritual harvest of grace, amidst the thorns and after the ploughings of temporal crosses.

The truth is, I never needed or desired more the service and assistance of men judiciously pious and soberly devout.

The solitude they have confined me unto adds the wilderness to my temptations: for the company they obtrude upon me is more sad than any solitude can be.

If I had asked my revenues, my power of the militia, or any one of my kingdoms, it had been no wonder to have been denied in those things, where the evil policy of men forbids all just restitution, lest they should confess an injurious usurpation: but to deny me the ghostly comfort of my chaplains, seems a greater rigour and barbarity than is ever used by Christians to the meanest prisoners and greatest malefactors; whom though the justice of the law deprives of worldly comforts, yet the mercy of religion allows them the benefit of their clergy, as not aiming at once to destroy their bodies and to damn their souls.

But my agony must not be relieved with the presence of any one good angel; for such I account a learned, godly, and discreet divine: and such I would have all mine to be.

They that envy my being a king, are loth I should be a Christian: while they seek to deprive me of all things else, they are afraid I should save my soul.

Other sense charity itself can hardly pick out of those many harsh repulses I received, as to that request so often made for the attendance of some of my chaplains.

I have sometimes thought, the unchristianness of those denials might arise from a displeasure some men had to see me prefer my own divines before their ministers: whom though I respect for that worth and piety which may be in them; yet I cannot think them so proper for my present comforters or physicians, who have (some of them at least) had so great an influence in occasioning these calamities, and inflicting these wounds upon me.

Nor are the soberest of them so apt for that devotional compliance and juncture of hearts, which I desire to bear in those holy offices to be performed with me and for me; since their judgments standing at a distance from me, or in jealousy of me, or in opposition against me, their spirits cannot so harmoniously accord with mine, or mine with theirs, either in prayer or other holy duties, as is meet and most comfortable; whose golden rule and bond of perfection consists in that of mutual love and charity.

Some remedies are worse than the disease, and some comforters more miserable than misery itself; when, like Job's friends, they seek not to fortify one's mind with patience, but persuade a man, by betraying his own innocency, to despair of God's mercy; and by justifying their injuries, to strengthen the hands and harden the hearts of insolent enemies.

I am so much a friend to all Churchmen that have anything in them beseeming that sacred function, that I have hazarded my own interest chiefly upon conscience and constancy to maintain their rights: whom the more I looked upon as orphans, and under the sacrilegious eyes of many cruel and rapacious reformers, the more I thought it my duty to appear as a father and a patron for them and the Church. Although I am very unhandsomely requited by some of them, who may live to repent no less for my sufferings than their own ungrateful errors, and that injurious contempt and meanness which they have brought upon their calling and persons.

I pity all of them, I despise none: only I thought I might have leave to make choice of some for my special attendants, who were best approved in my judgment, and most suitable to my affection. For I held it better to seem undevout, and to hear no men's prayers, than to be forced, or seem to comply with those petitions to which the heart cannot consent, nor the tongue say *Amen*, without contradicting a man's own understanding, or belying his own soul.

In devotions I love neither profane boldness, nor pious nonsense; but such an humble and judicious gravity, as shews the speaker to be at once considerate of God's majesty, the Church's honour, and his own vileness; both knowing what things God allows him to ask, and in what manner it becomes a sinner to supplicate the divine mercy for himself and others.

I am equally scandalized with all prayers that sound

either imperiously, or rudely, or passionately; as either wanting humility to God, or charity to men, or respect to the duty.

I confess I am better pleased, as with studied and premeditated sermons, so with such public forms of prayer as are fitted to the Church's and every Christian's daily and common necessities; because I am by them better assured what I may join my heart unto, than I can be of any man's extemporary sufficiency; which as I do not wholly exclude from public occasions, so I allow its just liberty and use in private and devout retirements, where neither the solemnity of the duty, nor the modest regard to others, do require so great exactness as to the outward manner of performance. Though the light of understanding and the fervency of affection, I hold the main and most necessary requisites both in constant and occasional, solitary and social devotions.

So that I must needs seem to all equal minds, with as much reason to prefer the service of my own chaplains before that of their ministers, as I do the Liturgy before their Directory.

In the one I have been always educated and exercised, in the other I am not yet catechised nor acquainted: and if I were, yet should I not by that, as by any certain rule and canon of devotion, be able to follow or find out the indirect extravagancies of most of those men who highly cry up as a piece of rare composure and use, which is already as much despised as disused by many of them, as the Common Prayer sometimes was by those men, a great part of whose piety hung upon that popular pin of railing against and contemning the government and Liturgy of this Church. But I had rather be condemned to the woe of *Væ soli*, than to that of *Væ vobis, Hypocritæ*, by seeming to pray what I do not approve.

It may be, I am esteemed by my deniers sufficient of myself to discharge my duty to God as a priest, though not to men as a prince.

Indeed I think both offices, regal and sacerdotal, might well become the same person; as anciently they were under one name, and the united rights of primogeniture: nor could I follow better precendents, if I were able, than those two eminent kings, David and Solomon; not more famous for their sceptres and crown, than one was for devout psalms and prayers, the other for his divine parables and preaching: whence the one merited and assumed the name of a prophet, the other of a preacher. Titles indeed of greater honour, where rightly placed, than any of those the Roman emperors affected from the nations they subdued; it being infinitely more glorious to convert souls to God's Church by the Word, than to conquer men to a subjection by the sword.

Yet since the order of God's wisdom and providence hath, for the most part, always distinguished the gifts and offices of kings and priests, of princes and preachers, both in the Jewish and Christian Churches; I am sorry to find myself reduced to the necessity of being both, or enjoying neither.

For such as seek to deprive me of my kingly power and sovereignty, would no less enforce me to live many months without all prayers, sacraments and sermons, unless I become my own chaplain.

As I owe the clergy the protection of a Christian king, so I desire to enjoy from them the benefit of their gifts and prayers; which I look upon as more prevalent than my own or other men's, by how much they flow from minds more enlightened and affections less distracted than those which are encumbered with secular affairs: besides, I think a greater blessing and acceptableness attends those duties, which are rightly performed, as proper to and within the limits of that calling to which God and the Church have specially designed and consecrated some men. And, however, as to that spiritual government by which the devout soul is subject to Christ, and through His merits daily offers itself and its services to God, every private believer is a king and a priest, invested with the honour of a royal priesthood; yet as to ecclesiastical order, and the outward polity of the Church, I think confusion in religion will as certainly follow every man's turning priest or preacher, as it will in the State where every one affects to rule as king.

I was always bred to more modest, and, I think, more pious principles: the consciousness to my spiritual defects makes me more prize and desire those pious assistances which holy and good ministers, either bishops or presbyters, may afford me; especially in these extremities to which God hath been pleased to suffer some of my subjects to reduce me so as to leave them nothing more but my life to take from me; and to leave me nothing to desire, which I thought might less provoke their jealousy and offence to deny me, than this, of having some means afforded me for my soul's comfort and support.

To which end I made choice of men, as no way (that I know) scandalous, so every way eminent for their learning and piety, no less than for their loyalty: nor can I imagine any exceptions to be made against them, but only this, that they may seem too able, and too well affected toward me and my service.

But this is not the first service (as I count it the best) in which they have forced me to serve myself: though I must confess, I bear with more grief and impatience the want of my chaplains than of any other my servants, and next, if not beyond in some things, to the being sequestered from my wife and 'children; since from these indeed more of human and temporary affections, but from those more of heavenly and eternal improvements, may be expected.

My comfort is, that in the enforced, not neglected want of ordinary means, God is wont to afford extraordinary supplies of His gifts and graces.

If His Spirit will teach me, and help my infirmities in prayer, reading and meditation, as I hope He will, I shall need no other either orator or instructor.

To Thee, therefore, O my God, do I direct my now solitary prayers: what I want of others' help, supply with the more immediate assistances of *Thy Spirit*, which alone can both enlighten my darkness and quicken my dulness.

O *Thou Sun of Righteousness*, *Thou sacred Fountain of heavenly light and heat*, at once clear and warm my heart, both by instructing of me and interceding for me. In *Thee* is all fulness, from *Thee* is all sufficiency, by *Thee* is all acceptance. *Thou* art company enough, and comfort enough: *Thou* art my *King*, be also my *Prophet* and my *Priest*. Rule me, teach me, pray in me, for me, and be *Thou* ever with me.

The single wrestlings of Jacob prevailed with *Thee* in that sacred duel, when he had none to second him but *Thyself*, who didst assist him with power to overcome *Thee*, and by a welcome violence to wrest a blessing from *Thee*.

O look on me, *Thy* servant, in infinite mercy, whom *Thou* didst once bless with the joint and sociated devotions of others, whose fervency might inflame the coldness of my affections towards *Thee*, when we went to or met in *Thy* house with the voice of joy and gladness, worshipping *Thee* in the unity of spirits, and with the bond of peace.

O forgive the neglect and not improving of those happy opportunities.

It is now *Thy* pleasure that I should be as a pelican in the wilderness, as a sparrow on the house-top, and as a coal scattered from all those pious glowings and devout reflections which might best kindle, preserve, and increase the holy fire of *Thy* graces on the altar of my heart, whence the sacrifice of prayers and the incense of praises might be duly offered up to *Thee*.

Yet, O Thou that breakest not the bruised reed nor quenchest the smoking flax, do not despise the weakness of my prayers nor the smotherings of my soul in this uncomfortable loneliness, to which I am constrained by some men's uncharitable denials of those helps which I much want and no less desire.

O let the hardness of their hearts occasion the softenings of mine to Thee and for them. Let their hatred kindle my love; let their unreasonable denials of my religious desires the more excite my prayers to Thee; let their inexorable deafness incline Thine ear to me, who art a God easy to be intreated: Thine ear is not heavy that it cannot, nor Thy heart hard, that it will not hear; nor Thy hand shortened, that it cannot help me Thy desolate suppliant.

Thou permittest men to deprive me of those outward means which Thou hast appointed in Thy Church, but they cannot debar me from the communion of that inward grace which Thou alone breathest into humble hearts.

O make me such, and Thou wilt teach me, Thou wilt hear me, Thou wilt help me: the broken and contrite heart, I know, Thou wilt not despise.

Thou, O Lord, canst at once make me Thy temple, Thy priest, Thy sacrifice, and Thine altar; while from an humble heart I (alone) daily offer up in holy meditations, fervent prayers, and unfeigned tears myself to Thee, who preparest me for Thee, dwellest in me, and acceptest of me.

Thou, O Lord, didst cause by secret supplies and miraculous infusions that the handful of meal in the *vessel should not spend, nor the little oil in the cruse fail the widow during the time of drought and dearth.*

O look on my soul, which, as a widow, is now desolate and forsaken: let not those saving truths I have formerly learned now fail my memory, nor the sweet effusions of Thy Spirit, which I have sometime felt, now be wanting to my heart in this famine of ordinary and wholesome food, for the refreshing of my soul.

Which yet I had rather choose, than to feed from those hands who mingle my bread with ashes and my wine with gall, rather tormenting than teaching me, whose mouths are proner to bitter reproaches of me than to hearty prayers for me.

Thou knowest, O Lord of truth, how oft they wrest Thy Holy Scriptures to my destruction, (which are clear for their subjection and my preservation); O let it not be to their damnation.

Thou knowest how some men, under colour of long prayers, have sought to devour the houses of their brethren, their King, and their God.

O let not those men's balms break my head, nor their cordials oppress my heart: I will evermore pray against their wickedness.

From the poison under their tongues, from the snares of their lips, from the fire and the swords of their words, ever deliver me, O Lord, and all those loyal and religious hearts who desire and delight in the prosperity of my soul, and who seek by their prayers to relieve this sadness and solitude of Thy servant, O my King and my God.

XXV.

PENITENTIAL MEDITATIONS AND VOWS IN THE KING'S SOLITUDE AT HOLDENBY.

Give ear to my words, O Lord, consider my meditation, and hearken to the voice of my cry, my King and my God, for unto Thee will I pray.

I said in mine haste, I am cast out of the sight of Thine eyes; nevertheless Thou hearest the voice of my supplication when I cry unto Thee.

If Thou, Lord, shouldst be extreme to mark what is done amiss, who can abide it? But there is mercy with Thee, that Thou mayest be feared; therefore shall sinners fly unto Thee.

I acknowledge my sins before Thee, which have the aggravation of my condition, the eminency of my place adding weight to my offence.

Forgive, I beseech Thee, my personal and my people's sins, which are so far mine, as I have not improved the power Thou gavest me to Thy glory and my subjects' good. Thou hast now brought me from the glory and freedom of a king to be a prisoner to my own subjects; justly, O Lord, as to Thy overruling hand, because in many things I have rebelled against Thee.

Though Thou hast restrained my person, yet enlarge my heart to Thee, and Thy grace towards me.

I come far short of David's piety; yet since I may equal David's afflictions, give me also the comforts and sure mercies of David.

Let the penitent sense I have of my sins be an evidence to me that Thou hast pardoned them.

Let not the evils which I and my kingdoms have suffered seem little unto Thee, though Thou hast not punished us according to our sins.

Turn Thee, O Lord, unto me: have mercy upon me, for I am desolate and afflicted.

The sorrows of my heart are enlarged: O bring Thou me out of my troubles.

Hast Thou forgotten to be gracious, and shut up Thy loving-kindness in displeasure?

O remember Thy compassions of old, and Thy loving-kindnesses which have been for many generations.

I had utterly fainted, if I had not believed to see Thy goodness in the land of the living.

Let not the sins of our prosperity deprive us of the benefit of Thy afflictions.

Let this fiery trial consume the dross which in long peace and plenty we had contracted.

Though Thou continuest miseries, yet withdraw not Thy grace: what is wanting of prosperity make up in patience and repentance.

And if Thy anger be not yet to be turned away, but Thy hand of justice must be stretched out still, let it, I beseech Thee, be against me and my father's house: as for these sheep, what have they done?

Let my sufferings satiate the malice of mine and Thy Church's enemies.

But let their cruelty never exceed the measure of my charity.

Banish from me all thoughts of revenge, that I may not lose the reward, nor Thou the glory of my patience.

As Thou givest me a heart to forgive them, so I beseech Thee do Thou forgive what they have done against Thee and me.

And now, O Lord, as Thou hast given me an heart to pray unto Thee, so hear and accept this vow which I make before Thee.

If Thou wilt in mercy remember me and my kingdoms in continuing the light of Thy Gospel, and settling Thy true religion among us;

In restoring to us the benefit of the laws and the due execution of justice;

In suppressing the many schisms in Church and factions in State:

If Thou wilt restore me and mine to the ancient rights and glory of my predecessors:

If Thou wilt turn the hearts of my people to Thyself in piety, to me in loyalty, and to one another in charity:

If Thou wilt quench the flames and withdraw the fuel of these civil wars:

If Thou wilt bless us with the freedom of public counsels, and deliver the honour of Parliaments from the insolency of the vulgar:

If Thou wilt keep me from the great offence of enacting anything against my conscience, and especially from consenting to sacrilegious rapines and spoilings of Thy Church:

If Thou wilt restore me to a capacity to glorify Thee in doing good both to the Church and State;

Then shall my soul praise Thee, and magnify Thy Name before my people:

Then shall Thy glory be dearer to me than my crowns, and the advancement of true religion both in purity and power be my chiefest care:

Then will I rule my people with justice, and my kingdoms with equity.

To Thy more immediate hand shall I ever owe, as the rightful succession, so the merciful restoration of my kingdoms, and the glory of them.

If Thou wilt bring me again with peace, safety, and honour, to my chiefest city and my Parliament:

If Thou wilt again put the sword of justice into my hand, to punish and protect:

Then will I make all the world to see, and my very enemies to enjoy, the benefit of this vow and resolution of Christian charity which I now make unto Thee, O Lord.

As I do freely pardon, for Christ's sake, those that have offended me in any kind, so my hand shall never be against any man, to revenge what is past, in regard of any particular injury done unto me.

We have been mutually punished in our unnatural divisions; for Thy sake, O Lord, and for the love of my Redeemer, have I purposed this in my heart, that I will use all means in the ways of amnesty and indemnity which may most fully remove all fears and bury all jealousies in forgetfulness.

Let Thy mercies be toward me and mine, as my resolutions of truth and peace are toward my people.

Hear my prayer, O Lord, which goeth not out of feigned lips.

Blessed be God, who hath not turned away my prayer nor taken His mercy from me.

O my soul, commit thy way to the Lord; trust in Him, and He shall bring it to pass.

But if Thou wilt not restore me and mine, what am I that I should charge Thee foolishly?

Thou, O Lord, hast given, and Thou hast taken; blessed be Thy Name.

May my people and Thy Church be happy, if not by me, yet without me.

XXVI.

UPON THE ARMY'S SURPRISAL OF THE KING AT HOLDENBY, AND THE ENSUING DISTRACTIONS IN THE TWO HOUSES, THE ARMY AND THE CITY.

WHAT part God will have me now to act or suffer in this new and strange scene of affairs I am not much solicitous. Some little practice will serve that man who only seeks to represent a part of honesty and honour.

This surprise of me tells the world that a king cannot be so low but he is considerable, adding weight to that party where he appears.

This motion, like others of the times, seems eccentric and irregular, yet not well to be resisted or quieted: better swim down such a stream, than in vain to strive against it.

These are but the strugglings of those twins which lately one womb enclosed, the younger striving to prevail against the elder; what the Presbyterians have hunted after, the Independents now seek to catch for themselves.

So impossible it is for lines to be drawn from the centre, and not to divide from each other so much the wider, by how much they go farther from the point of Union.

That the builders of Babel should from division fall to confusion, is no wonder; but for those that pretend to build Jerusalem, to divide their tongues and hands, is but an ill omen, and sounds too like the fury of those zealots whose intestine bitterness and divisions were the greatest occasion of the last fatal destruction of that city.

Well may I change my keepers and prison, but not my captive condition; only with this hope of bettering, that those who are so much professed patrons for the people's liberties cannot be utterly against the liberty of their King. What they demand for their own consciences, they cannot in reason deny to mine.

In this they seem more ingenuous than the Presbyterian rigour, who sometimes complaining of exacting their conformity to laws, are become the greatest exactors of other men's submission to their novel injunctions before they are stamped with the authority of laws, which they cannot well have without my consent.

It is a great argument that the Independents think

themselves manumitted from their rivals' service, in that they carry on a business of such consequence as the assuming my person into the Army's custody, without any commission but that of their own will and power. Such as will thus adventure on a King must not be thought over-modest or timorous to carry on any design they have a mind to.

Their next motion menaces and scares both the two Houses and the City, which soon after acting over again that former part or tumultuary motions (never questioned, punished, or repented), must now suffer for both, and see their former sin in the glass of the present terrors and distractions.

No man is so blind as not to see herein the hand of Divine justice: they that by tumults first occasioned the raising of armies, must now be chastened by their own army for new tumults.

So hardly can men be content with one sin, but add sin to sin, till the latter punish the former. Such as were content to see me and many members of both Houses driven away by the first unsuppressed tumults, are now forced to fly to an army, or defend themselves against them.

But who can unfold the riddle of some men's justice? The members of both Houses who at first withdrew (as myself was forced to do) from the rudeness of the tumults, were counted deserters, and outed of their places in Parliament; such as stayed then, and enjoyed the benefit of the tumults, were asserted for the only Parliament-men. Now the fliers from and forsakers of their places carry the Parliamentary power along with them, complain highly against the tumults, and vindicate themselves by an army; such as remained and kept their stations are looked upon as abettors of tumultuary insolencies, and betrayers of the freedom and honour of Parliament.

Thus is power above all rule, order, and law; where men look more to present advantages than their consciences, and the unchangeable rules of justice: while they are judges of others, they are forced to condemn themselves.

Now the plea against tumults holds good, the authors and abettors of them are guilty of prodigious insolencies, whenas before they were counted as friends and necessary assistants.

I see vengeance pursues and overtakes (as the mice and rats are said to have done a bishop in Germany) them that thought to have escaped, and fortified themselves most impregnably against it, both by their multitude and compliance.

Whom the laws cannot, God will punish by their own crimes and hands.

I cannot but observe this Divine justice, yet with sorrow and pity; for I always wished so well to Parliament and City, that I was sorry to see them do or suffer anything unworthy such great and considerable bodies in this kingdom.

I was glad to see them only scared and humbled, not broken by that shaking. I never had so ill a thought of those cities as to despair of their loyalty to me, which mistakes might eclipse, but I never believed malice had quite put out.

I pray God the storm be yet wholly passed over them; upon whom I look, as Christ did sometime over Jerusalem, as objects of my prayers and tears, with compassionate grief, foreseeing those severer scatterings which will certainly befall such as wantonly refuse to be gathered to their duty: fatal blindness frequently attending and punishing wilfulness, so that men shall not be able at last to prevent their sorrows who would not timely repent of their sins; nor shall they be suffered to enjoy the comforts who securely neglect the counsels belonging to their peace. They will find that brethren in iniquity are not far from becoming insolent enemies, there being nothing harder than to keep ill men long in one mind.

Nor is it possible to gain a fair period for those motions, which go rather in a round and circle of fancy than in a right line of reason tending to the law, the only centre of public consistency, whither I pray God at last bring all sides.

Which will easily be done, when we shall fully see how much more happy we are to be subject to the known laws than to the various wills of any men, seem they never so plausible at first.

Vulgar compliance with any illegal and extravagant ways, like violent motions in nature, soon grows weary of itself, and ends in a refractory sullenness: people's rebounds are often in their faces who first put them upon those violent strokes.

For the Army (which is so far excusable as they act according to soldiers' principles and interests, demanding pay and indemnity), I think it necessary, in order to the public peace, that they should be satisfied as far as is just, no man being more prone to consider them than myself. Though they have fought against me, yet I cannot but so far esteem that valour and gallantry they have sometime shewed, as to wish I may never want such men to maintain myself, my laws, and my kingdoms in such a peace as wherein they may enjoy their share and proportion as much as any men.

But Thou, O Lord, who art perfect unity in a sacred Trinity, in mercy behold those whom Thy justice hath divided.

Deliver me from the strivings of my people, and make me to see how much they need my prayers and pity, who agreed to fight against me, and yet are now ready to fight against one another, to the continuance of my kingdom's distractions.

Discover to all sides the ways of peace from which they have swerved, which consists not in the divided wills of parties, but in the joint and due observation of the laws.

Make me willing to go whither Thou wilt lead me by Thy providence; and be Thou ever with me, that I may see Thy constancy in the world's variety and changes.

Make me even such as thou wouldst have me, that I may at last enjoy that safety and tranquility which Thou alone canst give me.

Divert, I pray Thee, O Lord, Thy heavy wrath justly

hanging over those populous cities, whose plenty is prone to add fuel to their luxury, their wealth to make them wanton, their multitudes tempting them to security, and their security exposing them to unexpected miseries.

Give them eyes to see, hearts to consider, wills to embrace, and courage to act those things which belong to Thy glory and the public peace, lest their calamity come upon them as an armed man.

Teach them that they cannot want enemies who abound in sin, nor shall they be long undisarmed and undestroyed who with a high hand persisting to fight against Thee and the clear convictions of their own consciences, fight more against themselves than ever they did against me.

Their sins exposing them to Thy justice, their riches to others' injuries, their number to tumults, and their tumults to confusion.

Though they have with much forwardness helped to destroy me, yet let not my fall be their ruin.

Let me not so much consider either what they have done or I have suffered (chiefly at first by them) as to forget to imitate my crucified Redeemer, to plead their ignorance for their pardon; and in my dying extremities to pray to Thee, O Father, to forgive them, for they knew not what they did.

The tears they have denied me in my saddest condition, give them grace to bestow upon themselves; who the less they weep for me, the more cause they have to weep for themselves.

O let not my blood be upon them and their children, whom the fraud and faction of some, not the malice of all, have excited to crucify me.

But Thou, O Lord, canst and wilt (as Thou didst my Redeemer) both exalt and perfect me by my sufferings, which have more in them of Thy mercy than of man's cruelty or Thy own justice.

XXVII.

To the Prince of Wales.

Son, if these papers, with some others wherein I have set down the private reflections of my conscience and my most impartial thoughts touching the chief passages which have been most remarkable or disputed in my late troubles, come to your hands, to whom they are chiefly designed, they may be so far useful to you as to state your judgment aright in what hath passed; whereof a pious is the best use can be made; and they may also give you some directions how to remedy the present distempers, and prevent, if God will, the like for time to come.

It is some kind of deceiving and lessening the injury of my long restraint when I find my leisure and solitude have produced something worthy of myself and useful to you; that neither you nor any other may hereafter measure my cause by the success, nor my judgment of things by my misfortunes; which I count the greater by far because they have so far lighted upon you and some others whom I have most cause to love, as well as myself, and of whose unmerited sufferings I have a greater sense than of mine own.

But this advantage of wisdom you have above most

princes, that you have begun and now spent some years of discretion in the experience of troubles and exercise of patience; wherein piety and all virtues, both moral and political, are commonly better planted to a thriving, as trees set in winter, than in the warmth and serenity of times, or amidst those delights which usually attend princes' courts in times of peace and plenty; which are prone either to root up all plants of true virtue and honour, or to be contented only with some leaves and withering formalities of them, without any real fruits such as tend to the public good, for which princes should always remember they are born and by providence designed.

The evidence of which different education the Holy Writ affords us in the contemplation of David and Rehoboam, the one prepared by many afflictions for a flourishing kingdom, the other softened by the unparalleled prosperity of Solomon's court, and so corrupted to the great diminution both for peace, honour, and kingdom, by those flatteries which are as inseparable from prosperous princes as flies are from fruit in summer, whom adversity, like cold weather, drives away.

I had rather you should be Charles *le Bon* than *le Grand*, 'good' than 'great.' I hope God hath designed you to be both, having so early put you into the exercise of His graces and gifts bestowed upon you, which may best weed out all vicious inclinations and dispose you to those princely endowments and employments which may best gain the love and intend the welfare of those over whom God shall place you.

With God I would have you begin and end, who is King of kings, the Sovereign Disposer of the kingdoms of the world, who pulleth down one and setteth up another.

The best government and highest sovereignty you can attain to is to be subject to Him, that the sceptre of His Word and Spirit may rule in your heart.

The true glory of princes consists in advancing God's glory, in the maintenance of true religion and the Church's good, also in the dispensation of civil power with justice and honour to the public peace.

Piety will make you prosperous, at least it will keep you from being miserable; nor is he much a loser that loseth all, yet saveth his own soul at last.

To which centre of true happiness God, I trust, hath and will graciously direct all these black lines of affliction which He hath been pleased to draw on me, and by which He hath, I hope, drawn me nearer to Himself. You have already tasted of that cup whereof I have liberally drunk, which I look upon as God's physic, having that in healthfulness what it wants in pleasure.

Above all I would have you, as I hope you are already, well grounded and settled in your religion, the best profession of which I have ever esteemed that of the Church of England, in which you have been educated; yet I would have your own judgment and reason now seal to that sacred bond which education hath written, that it may be judiciously your own religion, and not other men's custom or tradition which you profess.

In this I charge you to persevere, as coming nearest to God's word for doctrine and to the primitive examples for government, with some little amendment, which I have otherwise expressed and often offered, though in vain. Your fixation in matters of religion will not be more necessary for your soul's than your kingdoms' peace, when God shall bring you to them.

For I have observed that the devil of rebellion doth commonly turn himself into an angel of reformation, and the old serpent can pretend new lights. When some men's consciences accuse them for sedition and faction, they stop its mouth with the name and noise of religion; when piety pleads for peace and patience, they cry out zeal.

So that unless in this point you be well settled, you shall never want temptations to destroy you and yours, under pretensions of reforming matters of religion, for that seems, even to the worst of men, as the best and most auspicious beginning of their worst designs.

Where besides the novelty, which is taking enough with the vulgar, every one hath an affectation, by seeming forward to an outward reformation of religion, to be thought zealous; hoping to cover those irreligious deformities whereto they are conscious by a severity of censuring other men's opinions or actions.

Take heed of abetting any factions, or applying to any public discriminations in matters of religion, contrary to what is in your judgment and the Church well settled. Your partial adhering, as head, to any one side, gains you not so great advantages in some men's hearts (who are prone to be of their king's religion) as it loseth you in others, who think themselves and their profession first despised, then persecuted by you. Take such a course as may either with calmness and charity quite remove the seeming differences and offences by impartiality, or so order affairs in point of power that you shall not need to fear or flatter any faction. For if ever you stand in need of them, or must stand to their courtesy, you are undone: the serpent will devour the dove. You may never expect less of loyalty, justice, or humanity, than from those who engage into religious rebellion; their interest is always made God's; under the colours of piety ambitious policies march, not only with greatest security, but applause as to the populacy: you may hear from them Jacob's voice, but you shall feel they have Esau's hands.

Nothing seemed less considerable than the Presbyterian faction in England for many years, so compliant they were to public order; nor, indeed, was their party great either in Church or State as to men's judgments. But as soon as discontents drove men into sidings, as ill humours fall to the disaffected part, which causeth inflammations, so did all at first who affected any novelties adhere to that side, as the most remarkable and specious note of difference then in point of religion.

All the lesser factions at first were officious servants to Presbytery, their great master, till time and military success, discovering to each their peculiar advantages, invited them to part stakes, and leaving the joint-stock of uniform religion, pretended each to drive for their party the trade of profits and preferments, to the breaking and undoing not only of the Church and State, but even of Presbytery itself, which seemed and hoped at first to have engrossed all.

Let nothing seem little or despicable to you in matters which concern religion and the Church's peace, so as to neglect a speedy reforming and effectual suppressing errors and schisms which seem at first but as a hand-breadth, yet by seditious spirits as by strong winds, are soon made to darken and cover the whole heaven.

When you have done justice to God, your own soul, and His Church, in the profession and preservation both of truth and unity in religion, the next main hinge on which your prosperity will depend and move is that of civil justice, wherein the settled laws of these kingdoms, to which you are rightly heir, are the most excellent rules you can govern by; which, by an admirable temperament,, gives very much to subjects' industry, liberty, and happiness, and yet reserve enough to the majesty and prerogative of any king who owns his people as subjects, not as slaves; whose subjection, as it preserves their property, peace, and safety, so it will never diminish your rights nor their ingenuous liberties, which consist in the enjoyment of the fruits of their industry and the benefit of those laws to which themselves have consented.

Never charge your head with such a crown as shall

by its heaviness oppress the whole body; the weakness of whose parts cannot return anything of strength, honour, or safety to the head, but a necessary debilitation and ruin.

Your prerogative is best shewed and exercised in remitting rather than exacting the rigour of the laws, there being nothing worse than legal tyranny.

In these two points, the preservation of established religion and laws, I may, without vanity, turn the reproach of my sufferings, as to the world's censure, into the honour of a kind of martyrdom, as to the testimony of my own conscience; the troublers of my kingdoms have nothing else to object against me but this, that I prefer religion and laws established before those alterations they propounded.

And so, indeed, I do and ever shall, till I am convinced by better arguments than what hitherto have been chiefly used towards me,—tumults, armies, and prisons.

I cannot yet learn that lesson, nor I hope ever will you, that it is safe for a king to gratify any faction with the perturbation of the laws, in which is wrapped up the public interest and the good of the community.

How God will deal with me as to the removal of these pressures and indignities which His justice by the very unjust hands of some of my subjects hath been pleased to lay upon me, I cannot tell; nor am I much solicitous what wrong I suffer from men, while I retain in my soul what I believe is right before God.

I have offered all for reformation and safety, that

in reason, honour, and conscience I can, reserving only what I cannot consent unto without an irreparable injury to my own soul, the Church, and my people, and to you also, as the next and undoubted heir of my kingdoms.

To which if the Divine Providence, to whom no difficulties are insuperable, shall in His due time after my decease bring you, as I hope He will, my counsel and charge to you is, that you seriously consider the former real or objected miscarriages which might occasion my troubles, that you may avoid them.

Never repose so much upon any man's single counsel, fidelity, and discretion in managing affairs of the first magnitude (that is, matters of religion and justice) as to create in yourself or others a diffidence of your own judgment, which is likely to be always more constant and impartial to the interest of your crown and kingdom than any man's.

Next, beware of exasperating any factions by the crossness and asperity of some men's passions, humours, or private opinions employed by you grounded only upon the differences in lesser matters, which are but the skirts and suburbs of religion.

Wherein a charitable connivance and Christian toleration often dissipates their strength whom rougher opposition fortifies, and puts the despised and oppressed party into such combinations as may most enable them to get a full revenge on those they count their persecutors, who are commonly assisted by that vulgar commiseration which attends all that are said to suffer under the notion of religion.

Provided the differences amount not to an insolent opposition of laws and government, or religion established, as to the essentials of them; such motions and minings are intolerable.

Always keep up solid piety, and those fundamental truths which mend both hearts and lives of men, with impartial favour and justice.

Take heed that outward circumstances and formalities of religion devour not all or the best encouragements of learning, industry, and piety; but with an equal eye and impartial hand distribute favours and rewards to all men, as you find them for their real goodness, both in abilities and fidelity, worthy and capable of them.

This will be sure to gain you the hearts of the best, and the most too; who, though they be not good themselves, yet are glad to see the severer ways of virtue at any time sweetened by temporal rewards.

I have, you see, conflicted with different and opposite factions, (for so I must needs call and count all those that act not in any conformity to the laws established in Church and State). No sooner have they by force subdued what they counted their common enemy, (that is, all those that adhered to the laws and to me,) and are secured from that fear, but they are divided into so high a rivalty as sets them more at defiance against each other than against their first antagonists.

Time will dissipate all factions, when once the rough horns of private men's covetous and ambitious designs shall discover themselves, which were at first wrapped up and hidden under the soft and smooth pretensions of religion, reformation, and liberty. As the wolf is not less cruel, so he will be more justly hated when he shall appear no better than a wolf under sheep's clothing.

But as for the seduced train of the vulgar, who in their simplicity follow those disguises, my charge and counsel to you is, that as you need no palliations for any designs (as other men) so that you study really to exceed (in true and constant demonstrations of goodness, piety, and virtue towards the people) even all those men that make the greatest noise and ostentations of religion; so you shall neither fear any detection (as they do who have but the face and mask of goodness); nor shall you frustrate the just expectations of your people, who cannot in reason promise themselves so much good from any subjects' novelties, as from the virtuous constancy of their king.

When these mountains of congealed factions shall, by the sunshine of God's mercy and the splendour of your virtues, be thawed and dissipated, and the abused vulgar shall have learned that none are greater oppressors of their estates, liberties, and consciences than those men that entitle themselves to patrons and vindicators of them, only to usurp power over them; let, then, no passion betray you to any study of revenge upon those whose own sin and folly will sufficiently punish them in due time.

But as soon as the forked arrow of factious emulations, is drawn out, use all princely arts and clemency to heal the wounds, that the smart of the cure may not equal the anguish of the hurt.

I have offered acts of indemnity and oblivion to so great a latitude, as may include all that can but suspect themselves to be any way obnoxious to the laws; and which might serve to exclude all future jealousies and insecurities.

I would have you always propense to the same way; whenever it shall be desired and expected, let it be granted, not only as an act of State policy and necessity, but of Christian charity and choice.

It is all I have now left me, a power to forgive those that have deprived me of all; and I thank God I have a heart to do it, and joy as much in this grace which God hath given me, as in all my former enjoyments; for this is a greater argument of God's love to me, than any prosperity can be.

Be confident, as I am, that the most of all sides who have done amiss have done so not out of malice, but mis-information or misapprehension of things.

None will be more loyal and faithful to me and you than those subjects who, sensible of their errors and our injuries, will feel in their own souls most vehement motives to repentance, and earnest desires to make some reparations for their former defects.

As your quality sets you beyond any duel with any subject, so the nobleness of your mind must raise you above the meditating any revenge, or executing your anger upon the many.

The more conscious you shall be to your own merits upon your people, the more prone you will be to expect all love and loyalty from them, and to inflict no punishment upon them for former miscarriages; you will have more inward complacency in pardoning one than in punishing a thousand.

This I write to you, not despairing of God's mercy and my subjects' affections towards you, both which I hope you will study to deserve; yet we cannot merit of God but by His own mercy.

If God shall see fit to restore me, and you after me, to those enjoyments which the laws have assigned to us, and no subjects without a high degree of guilt and sin can divest us of; then may I have better opportunity, when I shall be so happy to see you in peace, to let you more fully understand the things that belong to God's glory, your own honour, and the kingdom's peace.

But if you never see my face again, and God will have me buried in such a barbarous imprisonment and obscurity (which the perfecting some men's designs requires), wherein few hearts that love me are permitted to exchange a word or a look with me; I do require and entreat you, as your father and your King, that you never suffer your heart to receive the least check against or disaffection from the true religion established in the Church of England.

I tell you I have tried it, and after much search and many disputes have concluded it to be the best in the world; not only in the community, as Christian, but also in the special notion, as reformed; keeping middle way between the pomp of superstitious tyranny, and the meanness of fantastic anarchy.

Not but that (the draught being excellent as to the main, both for doctrine and government, in the Church of England) some lines, as in very good figures, may haply need some sweetening or polishing: which might here have easily been done by a safe and gentle hand, if some men's precipitancy had not violently demanded such rude alterations as would have quite destroyed all the beauty and proportions of the whole.

The scandal of the late troubles, which some may object and urge to you against the Protestant religion established in England, is easily answered to them or your own thoughts in this, that scarce any one who hath been a beginner, or an active prosecutor of this late war against the Church, the laws, and me, either was or is a true lover, embracer, or practiser, of the Protestant religion established in England; which neither gives such rules, nor ever before set such examples.

It is true some heretofore had the boldness to present threatening petitions to their princes and parliaments, which others of the same faction (but of worse spirits) have now put in execution. But let not counterfeit and disorderly zeal abate your value and esteem of true piety: both of them are to be *known by their fruits*. The sweetness of the vine and fig-tree is not to be despised, though the brambles and thorns should pretend to bear figs and grapes, thereby to rule over the trees.

Nor would I have you to entertain any aversion or dislike of parliaments, which in their right constitution, with freedom and honour, will never injure or diminish your greatness, but will rather be as interchangings of love, loyalty, and confidence between a prince and his people.

Nor would the events of this black parliament have been other than such, however much biassed by factions in the elections, if it had been preserved from the insolencies of popular dictates and tumultuary impressions; the sad effects of which will, no doubt, make all parliaments after this more cautious to preserve that freedom and honour which belongs to such assemblies, when once they have fully shaken off this yoke of vulgar encroachment, since the public interest consists in the mutual and common good both of prince and people.

Nothing can be more happy for all than in fair, grave, and honourable ways to contribute their counsels in common, enacting all things by public consent, without tyranny or tumults. We must not starve ourselves because some men have surfeited of wholesome food.

And if neither I nor you be ever restored to our rights, but God in His severest justice will punish my subjects with continuance in their sin, and suffer them to be deluded with the prosperity of their wickedness, I hope God will give me and you that grace which will teach and enable us to want as well as to wear a crown, which is not worth taking up or enjoying upon sordid, dishonourable, and irreligious terms.

Keep you to true principles of piety, virtue, and honour, you shall never want a kingdom.

A principal point of your honour will consist in your conferring all respect, love, and protection on your mother, my wife; who hath many ways deserved well of me, and chiefly in this, that (having been a means to bless me with so many hopeful children, all which, with their mother, I recommend to your love and care) she hath been content, with incomparable magnanimity and patience, to suffer both for and with me and you.

My prayer to God Almighty is, (whatever becomes of me, who am, I thank God, wrapt up and fortified in my own innocence and His grace,) that He would be pleased to make you an anchor, or harbour rather, to these tossed and weather-beaten kingdoms; a repairer, by your wisdom, justice, piety, and valour, of what the folly and wickedness of some men have so far ruined, as to leave nothing entire in Church or State, to the crown, the nobility, the clergy, or the commons, either as to laws, liberties, estates, order, honour, conscience, or lives.

When they have destroyed me (for I know not how far God may permit the malice and cruelty of my enemies to proceed, and such apprehensions some men's words and actions have already given me), as I doubt not but my blood will cry aloud for vengeance to Heaven, so I beseech God not to pour out His wrath upon the generality of the people, who have either deserted me or engaged against me, through the artifice and hypocrisy of their leaders, whose inward horror will be their first tormentor, nor will they escape exemplary judgments.

For those that loved me, I pray God they may have no miss of me when I am gone; so much I wish and hope that all good subjects may be satisfied with the blessings of your presence and virtues.

For those that repent of any defects in their duty toward me, as I freely forgive them in the word of a Christian King, so I believe you will find them truly zealous to repay with interest that loyalty and love to you which was due to me.

In sum, what good I intended, do you perform, when God shall give you power. Much good I have offered, more I purposed to Church and State, if times had been capable of it.

The deception will soon vanish, and the vizards will fall off apace. This mask of religion on the face of rebellion (for so it now plainly appears, since my restraint and cruel usage, that they fought not for me as was pretended) will not long serve to hide some men's deformities.

Happy times, I hope, attend you, wherein your subjects (by their miseries) will have learned, *That religion to their God, and loyalty to their King, cannot be parted, without both their sin and their infelicity.*

I pray God bless you, and establish your kingdoms

in righteousness, your soul in true religion, and your honour in the love of God and your people.

And if God will have disloyalty perfected by my destruction, let my memory ever with my name live in you, as of your father that loves you, and once a King of three flourishing kingdoms; whom God thought fit to honour not only with the sceptre and government of them, but also with the suffering many indignities and an untimely death for them, while I studied to preserve the rights of the Church, the power of the laws, the honour of my crown, the privilege of Parliaments, the liberties of my people, and my own conscience, which, I thank God, is dearer to me than a thousand kingdoms.

I know God can, I hope He yet will restore me to my rights; I cannot despair either of His mercy, or of my people's love and pity.

At worst, I trust I shall but go before you to a better kingdom, which God hath prepared for me, and me for it, through my Saviour Jesus Christ, to whose mercies I commend you and all mine.

Farewell till we meet, if not on earth, yet in heaven.

XXVIII.

MEDITATIONS UPON DEATH, AFTER THE VOTES OF NON-ADDRESSES, AND HIS MAJESTY'S CLOSER IMPRISONMENT IN CARISBROOK CASTLE.

As I have leisure enough, so I have cause more than enough to meditate upon and prepare for my death; for I know there are but few steps between the prisons and graves of princes.

It is God's indulgence which gives me the space, but man's cruelty that gives me the sad occasions for these thoughts.

For, besides the common burden of mortality, which lies upon me as a man, I now bear the heavy load of other men's ambitions, fears, jealousies, and cruel passions, whose envy or enmity against me makes their own lives seem deadly to them, while I enjoy any part of mine.

I thank God my prosperity made me not wholly a stranger to the contemplations of mortality: those are never unseasonable, since this is always uncertain, death being an eclipse which oft happeneth as well in clear as cloudy days.

But now my long and sharp adversity hath so reconciled in me those natural antipathies between life and death which are in all men, that, I thank God, the common terrors of it are dispelled, and the special horror of it, as to my particular, much allayed: for although my death at present may justly be represented to me with all those terrible aggravations which the policy of cruel and implacable enemies can put upon it, (affairs being drawn to the very dregs of malice); yet, I bless God, I can look upon all those stings as unpoisonous, though sharp, since my Redeemer hath either pulled them out, or given me the antidote of His death against them; which, as to the immaturity, unjustice, shame, scorn, and cruelty of it, exceeded whatever I can fear.

Indeed, I never did find so much the life of religion, the feast of a good conscience, and the brazen wall of a judicious integrity and constancy, as since I came to these closer conflicts with the thoughts of death.

I am not so old as to be weary of life, nor, I hope, so bad as to be either afraid to die, or ashamed to live. True, I am so afflicted, as might make me sometimes even desire to die, if I did not consider that it is the greatest glory of a Christian's life to *die daily*, in conquering, by a lively faith and patient hopes of a better life, those partial and quotidian deaths which kill us as it were, by piece-meals, and make us over-live our own fates; while we are deprived of health, honour, liberty, power, credit, safety, or estate, and those other comforts of dearest relations, which are as the life of our lives.

Though, as a King, I think myself to live in nothing temporal so much as in the love and goodwill of my people; for which, as I have suffered many deaths, so I hope that I am not in that point as yet wholly dead: notwithstanding my enemies have used all the poison of falsity and violence of hostility to destroy, first the love and loyalty which is in my subjects, and then all that content of life in me which from these I chiefly enjoyed.

Indeed, they have left me but little of life, and only the husk and shell, as it were, which their further malice and cruelty can take from me: having bereaved me of all those worldly comforts for which life itself seems desirable to men.

But, O my soul, think not that life too long or tedious wherein God gives thee any opportunities, if not to do, yet to suffer with such Christian patience and magnanimity in a good cause, as are the greatest honour of our lives, and the best improvement of our deaths.

I know that in point of true Christian valour it argues pusillanimity to desire to die out of weariness of life, and a want of that heroic greatness of spirit which becomes a Christian, in the patient and generous sustaining those afflictions which, as shadows, necessarily attend us while we are in this body, and which are lessened or enlarged as the sun of our prosperity moves higher or lower, whose total absence is best recompensed with the dew of heaven.

The assaults of affliction may be terrible, like Samson's lion, but they yield much sweetness to those that dare to encounter and overcome them; who know how to overlive the witherings of their gourds without discontent or peevishness, while they may yet converse with God.

That I must die as a man is certain: that I may die a King by the hands of my own subjects, a violent, sudden, and barbarous death, in the strength of my years, in the midst of my kingdoms, my friends and loving subjects being helpless spectators, my enemies insolent revilers and triumphers over me, living, dying, and dead, is so probable in human reason, that God hath taught me not to hope otherwise as to man's cruelty; however, I despair not of God's infinite mercy.

I know my life is the object of the devil's and wicked men's malice, but yet under God's sole custody and disposal: whom I do not think to flatter for longer life, by seeming prepared to die; but I humbly desire to depend upon Him, and to submit to His will both in life and death, in what order soever He is pleased to lay them out to me.

I confess it is not easy for me to contend with those many horrors of death wherewith God suffers me to be tempted; which are equally horrid either in the suddenness of a barbarous assassination, or in those greater formalities whereby my enemies (being more solemnly cruel) will, it may be, seek to add (as those did who crucified Christ) the mockery of justice to the cruelty of malice. That I may be destroyed, as with greater pomp and artifice so with less pity, it will be but a necessary policy to make my death appear as an act of justice done by subjects upon their sovereign; who know that no law of God or man invests them with any power of judicature without me, much less against me; and who, being sworn and bound by all that is sacred before God and man to endeavour my preservation, must pretend justice to cover their perjury.

It is indeed, a sad fate for any man to have his enemies to be his accusers, parties, and judges, but most desperate when this is acted by the insolence of subjects against their sovereign, wherein those who have had the chiefest hand, and are most guilty of contriving the public troubles, must by shedding my blood seem to wash their own hands of that innocent blood, whereof they are now most evidently guilty before God and man, and, I believe, in their own consciences too; while they carried on unreasonable demands, first by tumults, after by armies. Nothing makes mean spirits more cowardly cruel in managing their usurped power against their lawful superiors than this, the *guilt of their unjust usurpation:* notwithstanding those specious and popular pretensions of justice against delinquents, applied only to disguise at first the monstrousness of their designs, who despaired, indeed, of possessing the power and profits of the vineyard, till the heir whose right it is, be cast out and slain.

With them my greatest fault must be, that I would not either destroy myself, with the Church and State, by my word, or not suffer them to do it unresisted by the sword, whose covetous ambition no concessions of mine could ever yet either satisfy or abate.

Nor is it likely they will ever think that kingdom of brambles, which some men seek to erect (at once weak, sharp, and fruitless either to God or man), is like to thrive, till watered with the royal blood of those whose right the kingdom is.

Well, God's will be done. I doubt not but my innocence will find Him both my protector and my advocate, who is my only Judge; whom I own as King of kings, not only for the eminence of His power and majesty above them, but also for that singular care and protection which He hath over them; who knows them to be exposed to as many dangers (being the greatest patrons of law, justice, order, and religion on earth) as there be either men or devils which love confusion.

Nor will He suffer those men long to prosper in their Babel, who build it with the bones and cement it with the blood of their kings.

I am confident they will find avengers of my death among themselves: the injuries I have sustained from them shall be first punished by them, who agreed in nothing so much as in opposing me.

Their impatience to bear the loud cry of my blood, shall make them think no way better to expiate it than by shedding theirs who with them most thirsted after mine.

The sad confusions following my destruction are already presaged and confirmed to me by those I have lived to see since my troubles, in which God alone (who only could) hath many ways pleaded my cause, not suffering them to go unpunished whose confederacy in sin was their only security; who have cause to fear that God will both further divide, and by mutual vengeance afterward destroy them.

My greatest conquest of death is from the power and love of Christ, who hath swallowed up death in the victory of His Resurrection and the glory of His Ascension.

My next comfort is, that He give me not only the honour to imitate His example *in suffering for righteousness' sake* (though obscured by the foulest charges of tyranny and injustice), but also that charity, which is the noblest revenge upon and victory over my destroyers; by which, I thank God, I can both forgive them and pray for them, that God would not impute my blood to them, further than to convince them what need they have of Christ's blood to wash their souls from the guilt of shedding mine.

At present, the will of my enemies seems to be their only rule, their power the measure, and their success the exacter of what they please to call justice; while they flatter themselves with the fancy of their own safety by my danger, and the security of their lives and designs by my death; forgetting that as the greatest temptations to sin are wrapped up in seeming prosperities, so the severest vengeances of God are then most accomplished when men are suffered to complete their wicked purposes.

I bless God I pray not so much that this bitter cup of a violent death may pass from me, as that of His wrath may pass from all those whose hands by deserting me are sprinkled, or by acting and consenting to my death, are embrued with my blood.

The will of God hath confined and concluded mine: I shall have the pleasure of dying, without any pleasure of desired vengeance.

This, I think, becomes a Christian toward his enemies, and a King towards his subjects.

They cannot deprive me of more than I am content to lose, when God sees fit by their hands to take it from me; whose mercy, I believe, will more than infinitely recompense whatever by man's injustice He is pleased to deprive me of.

The glory attending my death will far surpass all I could enjoy or conceive in life.

I shall not want the heavy and envied crowns of this world, when my God hath mercifully crowned and consummated His graces with glory, and exchanged the shadows of my earthly kingdoms among men for the substance of that heavenly kingdom with Himself.

For the censures of the world, I know the sharp and necessary tyranny of my destroyers will sufficiently confute the calumnies of tyranny against me. I am persuaded I am happy in the judicious love of the ablest and best of my subjects, who do not only pity and pray for me, but would be content even to die with me or for me.

These know how to excuse my failings as a man, and yet to retain and pay their duty to me as their King; there being no religious necessity binding any subjects, by pretending to punish, infinitely to exceed the faults and errors of their princes, especially there where more than sufficient satisfaction had been made to the public, the enjoyment of which private ambitions have hitherto frustrated.

Others, I believe, of softer tempers and less advantaged by my ruin, do already feel sharp convictions and some remorse in their consciences; where they cannot but see the proportions of their evil dealings against me in the measure of God's retalliations upon them, who cannot hope long to enjoy their own thumbs and toes, having, under pretence of pairing others' nails, been so cruel as to cut off their chiefest strength.

The punishment of the more insolent and obstinate

may be like that of Korah and his complices (at once mutinying against both prince and priest), in such a method of Divine justice as is not ordinary; the earth of the lowest and meanest people opening upon them, and swallowing them up in a just disdain of their ill-gotten and worse used authority, upon whose support and strength they chiefly depended for their building and establishing their designs against me, the Church and State.

My chiefest comfort in death consists in my peace, which, I trust, is made with God; before whose exact tribunal I shall not fear to appear as to the cause so long disputed by the sword between me and my causeless enemies; where I doubt not but His righteous judgment will confute their fallacy, who from worldly success (rather like sophisters than sound Christians) draw those popular conclusions for God's approbation of their actions; whose wise Providence, we know, oft permits many events which His revealed Word (the only clear, safe, and fixed rule of good actions and good consciences) in no sort approves.

I am confident the justice of my cause and clearness of my conscience before God and toward my people will carry me as much above them in God's decision, as their successes have lifted them above me in the vulgar opinion: who consider not that many times those undertakings of men are lifted up to heaven in the prosperity and applause of the world, whose rise is from hell, as to the injuriousness and oppression of the design. The prosperous winds which oft fill the sails of pirates, do not justify their piracy and rapine.

I look upon it with infinite more content and quiet of soul, to have been worsted in my enforced contestation for and vindication of the laws of the land, the freedom and honour of Parliaments, the rights of my crown, the just liberty of my subjects, and the true Christian religion in its doctrine, government, and due encouragements, than if I had with the greatest advantages of success overborne them all, as some men have now evidently done, whatever designs they at first pretended.

The prayers and patience of my friends and loving subjects will contribute much to the sweetening of this bitter cup, which I doubt not but I shall more cheerfully take and drink as from God's hand (if it must be so), than they give it to me, whose hands are unjustly and barbarously lifted up against me.

And as to the last event, I may seem to owe more to my enemies than my friends; while those will put a period to the sins and sorrows attending this miserable life, wherewith these desire I might still contend.

I shall be more than conqueror through Christ enabling me for whom I have hitherto suffered, as He is the author of truth, order, and peace; for all which I have been forced to contend against error, faction, and confusion.

If I must suffer a violent death, with my Saviour, it is but mortality crowned with martyrdom: where the debt of death which I owe for sin to nature shall be raised as a gift of faith and patience offered to God.

Which I humbly beseech Him mercifully to accept: and although death be the wages of my own sin as from God, and the effect of others' sins as men, both against God and me, yet as I hope my own sins are so remitted that they shall be no ingredients to embitter the cup of my death, so I desire God to pardon their sins who are most guilty of my destruction.

The trophies of my charity will be more glorious and durable over them, than their ill-managed victories over me.

Though their sin be prosperous, yet they had need to be penitent, that they may be pardoned. Both which I pray God they may obtain; that my temporal death, unjustly inflicted by them, may not be revenged by God's just inflicting eternal death upon them: for I look upon the temporal destruction of the greatest king as far less deprecable than the eternal damnation of the meanest subject.

Nor do I wish other than the safe bringing of the ship to shore when they have cast me overboard; though it be very strange that mariners can find no other means to appease the storm themselves have raised but by drowning their pilot.

I thank God my enemies' cruelty cannot prevent my preparation; whose malice in this I shall defeat, that they shall not have the satisfaction to have destroyed my soul with my body: of whose salvation, while some of them have themselves seemed and taught others to despair, they have only discovered this, that they do not much desire it.

Whose uncharitable and cruel restraints, denying me even the assistance of any of my chaplains, hath rather enlarged than any way obstructed my access to the throne of heaven.

Where Thou dwellest, O King of Kings, who fillest heaven and earth, who art the fountain of eternal life, in whom is no shadow of death.

Thou, O God, art both the just inflictor of death upon us, and the merciful Saviour of us in it and from it.

Yea, it is better for us to be dead to ourselves and live in Thee, than by living in ourselves to be deprived of Thee.

O make the many bitter aggravations of my death, as a man and a King, the opportunities and advantages of Thy special graces and comforts in my soul as a Christian.

If Thou, Lord, wilt be with me, I shall neither fear nor feel any evil, though I walk through the valley of the shadow of death.

To contend with death is the work of a weak and mortal man; to overcome it is the grace of Thee alone, who art the Almighty and immortal God.

O my Saviour, who knowest what it is to die with me as a man, make me to know what it is to pass through death to life with Thee my God.

Though I die, yet I know that Thou my Redeemer livest for ever: though Thou slayest me, yet Thou hast encouraged me to trust in Thee for eternal life.

O withdraw not Thy favour from me, which is better than life.

O be not far from me, for I know not how near a violent and cruel death is to me.

As Thy omniscience, O God, discovers, so Thy omnipotence can defeat, the designs of those who have or shall conspire my destruction.

O shew me the goodness of Thy will, through the wickedness of theirs.

Thou givest me leave, as a man, to pray that this cup may pass from me; but Thou hast taught me as a Christian, by the example of Christ, to add, Not my will, but Thine be done.

Yea, Lord, let our wills be one, by wholly resolving mine into Thine: let not the desire of life in me be so great, as that of doing or suffering Thy will in either life or death.

As I believe Thou hast forgiven all the errors of my life, so I hope Thou wilt save me from the terrors of my death.

Make me content to leave the world's nothing, that I may come really to enjoy all in Thee, who hast made Christ unto me in life gain, and in death advantage.

Though my destroyers forget their duty to Thee, and me, yet do not Thou, O Lord, forget to be merciful to them.

For what profit is there in my blood, or in their gaining my kingdoms, if they lose their own souls?

Such as have not only resisted my just power, but wholly usurped and turned it against myself, though they may deserve, yet let them not receive to themselves damnation.

Thou madest Thy Son a Saviour to many that crucified Him, while at once He suffered violently by them, and yet willingly for them.

O let the voice of His Blood be heard for my murderers louder than the cry of mine against them.

Prepare them for Thy mercy by due convictions of their sin, and let them not at once deceive and damn their own souls by fallacious pretensions to justice in destroying me, while the conscience of their unjust usurpation of power against me chiefly tempts them to use all extremities against me.

O Lord, Thou knowest I have found their mercies to me as very false, so very cruel; who pretending to preserve me, have meditated nothing but my ruin.

O deal not with them as bloodthirsty and deceitful men, but overcome their cruelty with Thy compassion and my charity.

And when Thou makest inquisition for my blood, O sprinkle their polluted, yet penitent, souls with the Blood of Thy Son, that Thy destroying angel may pass over them.

Though they think my kingdoms on earth too little to entertain at once both them and me, yet let the capacious kingdom of Thy infinite mercy at last receive both me and my enemies.

When being reconciled to Thee in the Blood of the same Redeemer, we shall live far above these ambitious desires which beget such mortal enmities.

When their hands shall be heaviest and cruellest upon me, O let me fall into the arms of Thy tender and eternal mercies.

That what is cut off of my life in this miserable moment, may be repaid in Thy ever-blessed eternity.

Lord, let Thy servant depart in peace, for my eyes have seen Thy salvation.

VOTA DABUNT QUÆ BELLA NEGARUNT.

Private Prayers used by His Majesty in the Time of his Sufferings.

—:o:—

A Prayer in the Time of Captivity.

O POWERFUL and Eternal God, to whom nothing is so great that it may resist, or so small that it is contemned; look upon my misery with Thine eye of mercy, and let Thine infinite power vouchsafe to limit out some proportion of deliverance unto me as to Thee shall seem most convenient. Let not injury, O Lord, triumph over me, and let my faults by Thy hand be corrected; and make not my unjust enemies the ministers of thy justice: but yet, my God, if in Thy wisdom this be the aptest chastisement for my unexcusable transgressions, if this ungrateful bondage be fittest for my over-high desires; if the pride of my (not enough humble) heart be thus to be broken, O Lord, I yield unto Thy will, and cheerfully embrace what sorrow Thou wilt have me suffer: only thus much let me crave of Thee (let my craving, O Lord, be accepted of, since it even proceeds from Thee,) that by Thy goodness, which is Thyself, Thou wilt suffer some beam of Thy majesty so to shine in my mind, that I who in my greatest afflictions acknowledge it my noblest title to be Thy creature, may still depend confidently on Thee. Let calamity be the exercise, but not the overthrow of my virtue. O let not their prevailing power be to my destruction. And if it be Thy will that they more and more vex me with punishment, yet O Lord, never let their wickedness have such a hand, but that I may still carry a pure mind and steadfast resolution ever to serve Thee, without fear or presumption, yet with that humble confidence which may best please Thee; so that at the last I may come to Thy eternal kingdom, through the merits of Thy Son, our alone Saviour Jesus Christ. Amen.

Another Prayer.

ALMIGHTY and most merciful Father, look down upon me Thy unworthy servant, who here prostrate myself at the footstool of Thy throne of grace; but look upon me O Father, through the mediation and the merits of Jesus Christ, in whom Thou art only well pleased; for, of myself, I am not worthy to stand before Thee, or to speak with my unclean lips to Thee, most holy and eternal God; for as in sin I was conceived and born, so likewise I have broken all Thy commandments by my sinful motions, unclean thoughts, evil words, and wicked works; omitting many duties I ought to do, and committing many vices which Thou hast forbidden under pain of Thy heavy displeasure. As for my sins, O Lord, they are innumerable; wherefore I stand here liable to all the miseries in this life, and everlasting torments in that to come, if Thou shouldst deal with me according to my deserts. I confess, O Lord, that it is Thy mercy (which endureth for ever) and

Thy compassion (which never fails), which is the cause that I have not been long ago consumed: but with Thee there is mercy and plenteous redemption; in the multitude therefore of Thy mercies, and by the merits of Jesus Christ, I entreat Thy Divine Majesty that Thou wouldst not enter into judgment with Thy servant, nor be extreme to mark what is done amiss; but be Thou merciful unto me, and wash away all my sins with that precious Blood that my Saviour shed for me. And I beseech Thee, O Lord, not only to wash away all my sins, but also to purge my heart by Thy Holy Spirit from the dross of my natural corruption; and as Thou dost add days to my life, so, good Lord, I beseech Thee to add repentance to my days, that when I have past this mortal life, I may be partaker of Thy everlasting kingdom, through the merits of Jesus Christ our Lord. Amen.

A Prayer and Confession, made in and for the Times of Affliction.

ALMIGHTY and most merciful Father, as it is only Thy goodness that admits of our imperfect prayers, and the knowledge that Thy mercies are infinite, which can give us any hope of Thy accepting or granting them; so it is our bounden and necessary duty to confess our sins freely unto Thee; and of all men living I have most need, most reason so to do, no man having been so much obliged by Thee, no man more grievously offending Thee, that degree of knowledge which Thou hast given me adding likewise to the guilt of my transgressions. For was it through ignorance that I suffered innocent blood to be shed by a false pretended way of justice? or that I permitted a wrong way of Thy worship to be set up in Scotland, and injured the bishops in England? Oh, no; but with shame and grief I confess that I therein followed the persuasions of worldly wisdom, forsaking the dictates of a right-informed conscience; wherefore, O Lord, I have no excuse to make, no hope left, but in the multitude of Thy mercies, for I know my repentance weak, and my prayers faulty. Grant, therefore, merciful Father, so to strengthen my repentance and amend my prayers, that Thou mayest clear the way for Thine own mercies, to which O let Thy justice at last give place, putting a speedy end to my deserved afflictions. In the meantime give me patience to endure constancy against temptations, and a discerning spirit to choose what is best for Thy Church and people which Thou hast committed to my charge. Grant this, O most merciful Father, for Thy Son Jesus Christ's sake, our only Saviour. Amen.

A Prayer in Time of imminent Danger.

O MOST merciful Father, though my sins are so many and grievous that I may rather expect the effects of Thy anger than so great a deliverance as to free me from my present great danger, yet, O Lord, since Thy mercies are over all Thy works, and Thou never failest to relieve all those who with humble and unfeigned repentance come to Thee for succour, it were to multiply, not diminish my transgressions to despair of Thy heavenly favour: wherefore I humbly desire Thy Divine Majesty that Thou wilt not only pardon all my sins, but also free me out of the hands and protect me from the malice of my cruel enemies. But if Thy wrath against my heinous offences will not otherwise be satisfied than by suffering me to fall under my present afflictions, Thy will be done. Yet with humble importunity I do, and shall never leave to implore the assistance of Thy heavenly Spirit, that my cause, as I am Thy vicegerent, may not suffer through my weakness or want of courage. O Lord, so strengthen and enlighten all the faculties of my mind, that with clearness I may show forth Thy truth, and manfully endure this bloody trial; that so my sufferings here may not only glorify Thee, but likewise be a furtherance to my salvation hereafter. Grant this, O merciful Father, for His sake who suffered for me, even Jesus Christ the righteous. Amen.

www.ingramcontent.com/pod-product-compliance
Lightning Source LLC
Chambersburg PA
CBHW031936230426
43672CB00010B/1939